Geometry Workshop

Preparation for the Geometry Section of Standardized Tests

A self-teaching program to help improve mathematics skills that are tested on
- *Standardized tests* such as the Iowa, CAT, SRA, MAT and ERB.
- *College admission tests* such as the SAT and ACT.

by
Edward Williams

with
Elinor R. Ford, Ed.D.

Editorial Consultants

Kenneth Goldberg, Ph.D.
Professor of Mathematics Education
New York University
New York, New York

Sondra Reger
South Carroll High School
Sykesville, Maryland

Sadlier-Oxford
A Division of William H. Sadlier, Inc.
New York
Chicago
Los Angeles

Contents

Home Office:
9 Pine Street
New York, NY 10005

ISBN: 0-87105-472-8
23456789/9876543

What Is
Geometry Workshop?

You have been preparing for Achievement and Aptitude Tests in all your mathematics courses. Most students need practice–study materials to review concepts found in the Geometry Section of these tests. GEOMETRY WORKSHOP is designed to help you prepare for all types of standardized tests.

The tests in this book are very much like the geometry section of an actual test. The *real* test and each *practice* test have the very same

- types of questions
- level of difficulty

Furthermore, there are special features in GEOMETRY WORKSHOP that will GET YOU READY for the actual test:

1. Diagnostic Tests with Sample Answer Sheets
These tests are designed to pinpoint students' weaknesses in the ten major areas of geometry.
- 40 questions on each test
- Answers keyed to Refresher Sections for quick reference to study materials

2. Geometry Refresher Sections with Problem Solving
The Geometry Refresher Sections provide a carefully developed review of concepts and skills in geometry.

- Angles
- Lines
- Polygons
- Triangles
- Circles
- Perimeter
- Area
- Volume
- Coordinate Geometry
- Problem Solving

3. Practice Tests
Practice Tests for each of the ten areas found in the Geometry Refresher Section.

- Angles Test
- Lines Test
- Polygons Test
- Triangles Test
- Circles Test
- Perimeter Test
- Area Test
- Volume Test
- Coordinate Geometry Test
- Problem Solving Test
- Complete step-by-step solutions
- Answers keyed to Refresher Sections for quick reference to study materials
- *Error Analysis* for each test item

4. Two Sample SAT-Type Geometry Tests
- 30 questions on each test
- Complete step-by-step solutions
- Answers keyed to Refresher Sections for quick reference to study materials
- Selected *Error Analysis* for each test

How the Geometry Workshop Works

The special features of the GEOMETRY WORKSHOP are
- clear, concise presentations of solutions
- selected error analysis for self-improvement

Example:

Right isosceles triangle DEF and square BCDF share a common side DF. If the area of the square is 64, then the perimeter of BCDEF is

(A) $28\sqrt{2}$ (B) $24 + 8\sqrt{2}$

(C) $32\sqrt{2}$ (D) $32 + 8\sqrt{2}$

(E) $40\sqrt{2}$

Solution:

(B) If the area of square BCDF is 64, then

$$A = s^2$$
$$64 = s^2$$
$$8 = s$$

Therefore, BC = CD = DF = FB = 8.

DEF is a 45-45-90 triangle with hypotenuse DF = 8. The measure of either of the congruent legs is equal to the product of $\frac{1}{2}$ the measure of the hypotenuse and $\sqrt{2}$. Thus, DE = EF = $\frac{1}{2}(8)\sqrt{2}$ = $4\sqrt{2}$.

The perimeter of BCDEF is

$$P = CD + DE + EF + FB + BC$$
$$P = 8 + 4\sqrt{2} + 4\sqrt{2} + 8 + 8 = 24 + 8\sqrt{2}$$

Error Analysis:

If your choice was

(A), you forgot to include either DE or EF in the perimeter and combined $24 + 4\sqrt{2}$.

(C), you found the correct answer but combined $24 + 8\sqrt{2}$.

(D), you added in side DF.

(E), see (D) above and you combined $32 + 8\sqrt{2}$.

- For additional help, see Geometry Refresher Sections 7.1, 4.8, and 6.1 beginning on page 23.
- For further help, see Perimeter Test on page 84.
- For further preparation in mathematics for standardized tests, use the other books in this series.

Arithmetic Workshop
Algebra Workshop
Mathematics Workshop — Preparation for the
Mathematics Section of the SAT

Types of
Multiple-Choice Questions

There are two types of multiple-choice questions used in the mathematics section of standardized tests: the standard multiple-choice questions and quantitative comparison questions.

The standard multiple-choice questions offer 5 choices as solutions, but only 4 choices are given in the quantitative comparison questions.

● **Standard Multiple-Choice Questions**
These questions are familiar to most students. A problem is presented with 5 possible answer choices and you are to solve the problem and select the best of the choices given. Then you are to blacken in the space on the answer sheet corresponding to your answer choice.

EXAMPLE: If $a = 2 \cdot 3 \cdot 5$ and $b = 2 \cdot 3$, then $a + b$ is equal to the product of 6 and

(A) 5   (B) 6   (C) 1   (D) -6 (E) -5

Since $a = 2 \cdot 3 \cdot 5$ and $b = 2 \cdot 3$,
then $a = 30$ and $b = 6$.

So
$$a + b = 6 \cdot n \quad \text{(Missing factor)}$$
$$30 + 6 = 6n$$
$$36 = 6n$$
$$6 = n$$

Answer B is the best choice, so blacken circle B on the answer sheet.   (A) ● (C) (D) (E)

● **Quantitative Comparison Questions**
You may not be as familiar with this type of problem as you are with standard multiple-choice questions. Quantitative comparison questions require the use of estimation skills and an understanding of inequalities. Less computation and reading are needed to answer them, but critical thinking is essential. In order to improve your skills, be sure you understand the directions and practice solving as many quantitative comparison questions as possible.

To solve a quantitative comparison problem, you compare the quantities in the two columns and decide whether one quantity is greater than the other, whether the two quantities are equal, or whether the comparison cannot be determined from the information given.

The directions and notes are reprinted here exactly as they will appear on the actual Scholastic Aptitude Test.

**Directions:* Each of the following questions consists of two quantities, one in Column A and one in Column B. You are to compare the two quantities and on the answer sheet blacken space

A if the quantity in Column A is greater;
B if the quantity in Column B is greater;
C if the two quantities are equal;
D if the relationship cannot be determined from the information given.

An E response will not be scored.

Notes:

1. In certain questions, information concerning one or both of the quantities to be compared is centered above the two columns.
2. In a given question, a symbol that appears in both columns represents the same thing in Column A as it does in Column B.
3. Letters such as x, n, and k stand for real numbers.

EXAMPLE:

Column A	*Column B*
$x * y$ is defined as $\frac{x+y}{x}$	
$6 * 3$	$4 * 2$

If $x * y = \frac{x+y}{x}$,

then $6 * 3 = \frac{6+3}{6} = \frac{9}{6}$ or $\frac{3}{2}$

$4 * 2 = \frac{4+2}{4} = \frac{6}{4}$ or $\frac{3}{2}$

Since $6 * 3$ and $4 * 2$ are equal, space C is blackened.

Answers: Ⓐ Ⓑ ● Ⓓ Ⓔ

Since these questions have four answer choices, A, B, C, and D, you must be careful not to mark E as an answer.

If additional information or diagrams are needed, it will appear above the quantities to be compared.

*Directions reprinted with permission of Educational Testing Service, the copyright owner. From *Taking the SAT, 1986-87*; College Entrance Examination Board, New York. This booklet describes the tests, gives tips on test-taking strategies, and explains the different kinds of questions. The booklet may be obtained on request by writing to the College Board ATP, CN 6200, Princeton, NJ 08541-6200.

Test-Taking Tips

Preparing for the Test

To make sure you are prepared for the test, you should
1. be familiar with its organization
2. know the types of questions that will appear on it
3. know what is expected of you on the test day

1. Be Familiar with its Organization
- Is there more than one part to the test?
- Is there a time limit for the entire test?
- Is there a time limit for each part?
- How many questions are there in all?
- Do I need special tools for the test?
- Can a calculator be used during the test?
- Will there be a separate answer sheet?
- How many choices for answers will there be?
- How do I mark my answer on the answer sheet?
- Will I gain or lose points if I omit an answer?
- Is there a penalty for guessing an answer?

2. Know the Types of Questions
- Will there be standard multiple-choice questions?
- Will there be quantitative comparison questions?
- Will there be another type of question on the test with which I am not familiar?
- Are sample tests available with which I can practice?

Read and study the information on *Types of Multiple-Choice Questions* found on pp. 5-6, in this book.

3. What is Expected on the Test Day
- Do I know the location of the testing center?
- Do I know the time of the examination?
- How much time will I need to travel to the testing center?
- Did I bring the tools, if any, that are needed for the test?
- Do I need an admissions ticket?
- Do I need acceptable identification?
- Did I get a good night's sleep?
- Do I feel well prepared to take the test?

During the Test

To make sure you score as high as you can on the test,
you should
1. read the question carefully
2. search out groups of questions of the same type
3. estimate before you actually complete the answer
4. use an *educated* guess

1. Read the Question Carefully
- Do I understand the directions for the question?
- Do I know what is being asked in the question?
- Have I reread the question to be sure that I have answered it?
- Is my answer reasonable?

2. Group Questions of the Same Type
- Did I look for the questions I know how to do and complete these first?
- Did I mark off with an X through the number of the question, those questions which I know how to do and have completed.
- Did I mark off with a / through the number of the question, those questions of which I am not sure but have completed?
- Did I leave unmarked, the numbers of the questions I did not answer and must return to later?

3. Estimate the Answer
- Is my computed answer reasonable when compared to my estimated answer?
- If my computed answer and estimated answer do not correspond, do I know which is correct?
- Is there an alternative method I can use to solve the problem?

4. Use an *Educated* Guess
- Can I estimate the answer without doing the actual computation?
- Can I eliminate as definitely wrong one or more choices for the answer?
- Can I, fairly accurately, choose the correct answer from the remaining choices?

Part One

Two Diagnostic Tests

This section contains two Diagnostic Tests designed to help pinpoint weaknesses in ten areas of geometry. These areas are

- Angles
- Lines
- Polygons
- Triangles
- Circles
- Perimeter
- Area
- Volume
- Coordinate Geometry
- Problem Solving

Use the Answer Sheet that precedes each test to record your answers. The Answer Sheet for Test 1 is found on page 10, and the Answer Sheet for Test 2 is on page 16.

After you have completed each test, you can check your answers using the Answer Key on page 22.

If you need additional help, each answer is referenced (in parentheses) to the appropriate Geometry Refresher Section.

Answer Sheet

Diagnostic Test 1

ANGLES

1. Ⓐ Ⓑ Ⓒ Ⓓ
2. Ⓐ Ⓑ Ⓒ Ⓓ
3. Ⓐ Ⓑ Ⓒ Ⓓ
4. Ⓐ Ⓑ Ⓒ Ⓓ

LINES

5. Ⓐ Ⓑ Ⓒ Ⓓ
6. Ⓐ Ⓑ Ⓒ Ⓓ
7. Ⓐ Ⓑ Ⓒ Ⓓ
8. Ⓐ Ⓑ Ⓒ Ⓓ

POLYGONS

9. Ⓐ Ⓑ Ⓒ Ⓓ
10. Ⓐ Ⓑ Ⓒ Ⓓ
11. Ⓐ Ⓑ Ⓒ Ⓓ
12. Ⓐ Ⓑ Ⓒ Ⓓ

TRIANGLES

13. Ⓐ Ⓑ Ⓒ Ⓓ
14. Ⓐ Ⓑ Ⓒ Ⓓ
15. Ⓐ Ⓑ Ⓒ Ⓓ
16. Ⓐ Ⓑ Ⓒ Ⓓ

CIRCLES

17. Ⓐ Ⓑ Ⓒ Ⓓ
18. Ⓐ Ⓑ Ⓒ Ⓓ
19. Ⓐ Ⓑ Ⓒ Ⓓ
20. Ⓐ Ⓑ Ⓒ Ⓓ

PERIMETER

21. Ⓐ Ⓑ Ⓒ Ⓓ
22. Ⓐ Ⓑ Ⓒ Ⓓ
23. Ⓐ Ⓑ Ⓒ Ⓓ
24. Ⓐ Ⓑ Ⓒ Ⓓ

AREA

25. Ⓐ Ⓑ Ⓒ Ⓓ
26. Ⓐ Ⓑ Ⓒ Ⓓ
27. Ⓐ Ⓑ Ⓒ Ⓓ
28. Ⓐ Ⓑ Ⓒ Ⓓ

VOLUME

29. Ⓐ Ⓑ Ⓒ Ⓓ
30. Ⓐ Ⓑ Ⓒ Ⓓ
31. Ⓐ Ⓑ Ⓒ Ⓓ
32. Ⓐ Ⓑ Ⓒ Ⓓ

COORDINATE GEOMETRY

33. Ⓐ Ⓑ Ⓒ Ⓓ
34. Ⓐ Ⓑ Ⓒ Ⓓ
35. Ⓐ Ⓑ Ⓒ Ⓓ
36. Ⓐ Ⓑ Ⓒ Ⓓ

PROBLEM SOLVING

37. Ⓐ Ⓑ Ⓒ Ⓓ
38. Ⓐ Ⓑ Ⓒ Ⓓ
39. Ⓐ Ⓑ Ⓒ Ⓓ
40. Ⓐ Ⓑ Ⓒ Ⓓ

Diagnostic Test 1

Directions:
Solve each problem in this Diagnostic Test. Use any available space on the page for scratchwork. Then decide which is the best of the choices given and either darken the corresponding space on the Answer Sheet on page 10 or circle your answer from among the choices provided.

ANGLES

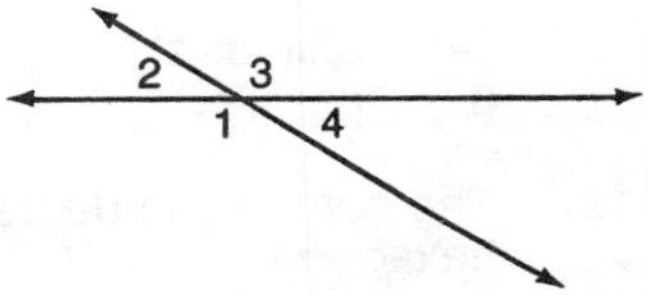

1. In the figure at the right, which angles form a pair of vertical angles?

   (A) $\angle 1, \angle 2$ (B) $\angle 2, \angle 3$
   (C) $\angle 3, \angle 4$ (D) $\angle 2, \angle 4$

2. If two angles are complementary, then the sum of their degree measures is

   (A) 60   (B) 90   (C) 180   (D) 360

Questions 3-4 refer to the diagram at the right.

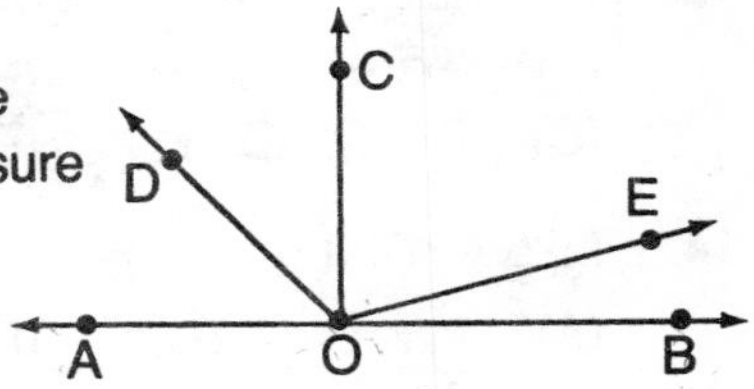

3. Points A, O, and B lie along a straight line and $\overrightarrow{OC}$ bisects $\angle AOB$. The degree measure of $\angle COB$ is

   (A) 45   (B) 90
   (C) 135   (D) 180

4. If $\overrightarrow{OD}$ bisects $\angle AOC$, then which of the following must be true?

   (A) $\angle COE \cong \angle EOB$ (B) $\angle AOD$ is complementary to $\angle BOE$
   (C) $\angle DOC \cong \angle COE$ (D) $\angle AOD \cong \angle DOC$

LINES

5. The number of lines that pass through two distinct points is

   (A) 0   (B) 1   (C) 2   (D) 3

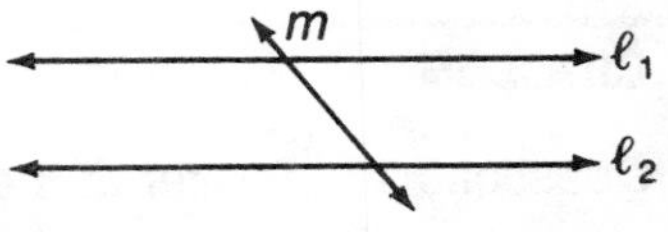

6. In the figure at the right, line m is

   (A) a bisector   (B) parallel
   (C) a transversal   (D) perpendicular

7. If two lines are perpendicular, then they intersect in how many points?

   (A) 0   (B) 1   (C) 2   (D) 3

8. If $\ell_1 \parallel \ell_2 \parallel \ell_3$ and $\ell_3 \perp \ell_4$, then

   (A) $\ell_1 \perp \ell_4$ (B) $\ell_2 \parallel \ell_4$ (C) $\ell_1 \perp \ell_3$ (D) $\ell_1 \parallel \ell_4$

POLYGONS

9. If two polygons have the same shape and the same size, the polygons must be

(A) similar   (B) congruent
(C) regular   (D) equilateral

10. The number of sides a decagon has is

(A) 6   (B) 8   (C) 10   (D) 12

11. In a rectangle, the diagonals are

(A) altitudes   (B) perpendicular
(C) parallel   (D) congruent

12. The sum of the degree measures of all the interior angles of a hexagon is

(A) 540   (B) 720   (C) 1080   (D) 1440

TRIANGLES

13. In $\triangle ABC$, if $\angle A \cong \angle B$, then

(A) $\overline{AC} \cong \overline{BC}$ (B) $\overline{AB} \cong \overline{AC}$
(C) $\overline{BC} \cong \overline{AB}$ (D) $AC > BC$

14. In $\triangle ABC$, if $m \angle A = 30°$ and $m \angle B = 75°$, then

(A) $m \angle C = 105°$ (B) $\overline{AB} \cong \overline{AC}$
(C) $\overline{AB} \cong \overline{BC}$ (D) $m \angle C = 70°$

15. If $\triangle XYZ$ is equilateral, then $m \angle Y =$

(A) 15°   (B) 30°   (C) 45°   (D) 60°

16. In the figure at the right, if $\overline{PQ} \cong \overline{QR}$, then $\overline{NQ}$ is a(n)

(A) altitude   (B) angle bisector
(C) median   (D) leg

CIRCLES

Questions 17-19 refer to the figure at the right.

17. Which line segment is a diameter?

(A) AD   (B) AO
(C) AC   (D) EC

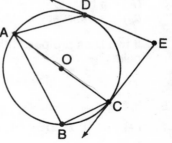

18. The m ∠ ACE =

(A) 30°   (B) 45°
(C) 60°   (D) 90°

19. Which line segments are congruent?

(A) AD and AB   (B) AO and BC
(C) ED and EC   (D) AB and AC

20. In the figure at the right, m$\overparen{BC}$ =

(A) 20°   (B) 30°
(C) 40°   (D) 60°

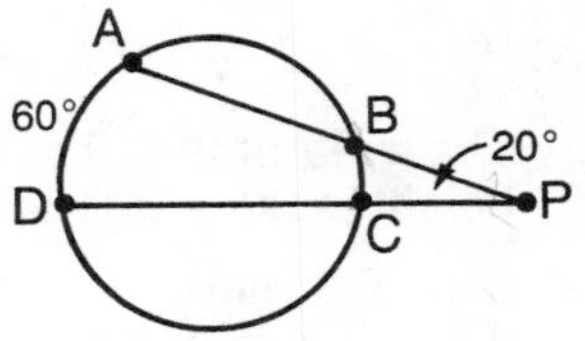

PERIMETER

21. If the perimeter of a square is 60, the length of each side is

(A) 12   (B) 15   (C) 20   (D) 30

22. If the base of an isosceles triangle is 10 and the perimeter is 40, then the length of a side of the triangle is

(A) 10   (B) 15   (C) 20   (D) 30

23. If each side of a regular hexagon is 6, the perimeter is

(A) 24   (B) 30   (C) 36   (D) 48

24. The width of a rectangle is w and the length is 7. If the perimeter is 21, the ratio of the width to the length is

(A) $\frac{1}{4}$ (B) $\frac{1}{3}$ (C) $\frac{3}{7}$ (D) $\frac{1}{2}$

AREA

25. If the base and altitude of a triangle are 4 and 5 respectively, the area of the triangle is

(A) 9   (B) 10   (C) 15   (D) 20

26. If the diameter of a circle is 8, the area is

(A) 8π   (B) 16   (C) 16π   (D) 64π

27. If each side of a square is 16, the area is

(A) 4   (B) 16   (C) 64   (D) 256

28. If the length of a rectangle is twice the width and the area is 72, then the width is

(A) 6   (B) 18   (C) 24   (D) 576

VOLUME

29. If each edge of a cube is 3, the volume is

(A) 6   (B) 9   (C) 12   (D) 27

30. If the dimensions of a rectangular prism are 2 by 3 by 4, the volume is

(A) 9   (B) 24   (C) 48   (D) 58

31. The area of the base of a rectangular prism is 189 mm² and its height is 30 mm. The volume is

(A) 6.3 mm³   (B) 219 mm³
(C) 567 mm³   (D) 5670 mm³

32. If the radius of the base of a cylinder is 6 and the height is 3, the volume is

(A) 18π (B) 27π (C) 54π (D) 108π

COORDINATE GEOMETRY

33. For a point below the x-axis and to the left of the y-axis,

(A) $x < 0, y < 0$ (B) $x < 0, y > 0$
(C) $x > 0, y < 0$ (D) $x > 0, y > 0$

34. Points $(3, y_1)$ and $(3, y_2)$ lie

(A) on the same horizontal line
(B) on the same vertical line
(C) on the same point
(D) It cannot be determined from the information given.

35. The distance between (1, 4) and (4, 8) is

(A) 2   (B) 3
(C) 4   (D) 5

36. In the figure at the right, which point has coordinates (3, −1)?

(A) P
(B) Q
(C) R
(D) S

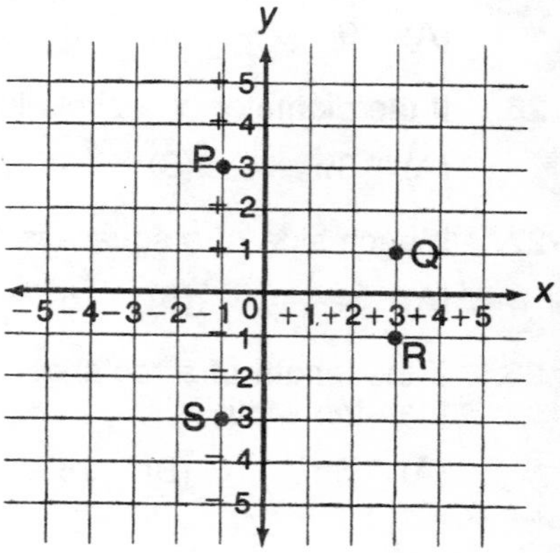

PROBLEM SOLVING

37. In the figure at the right, the area of the square is 1. The area of the shaded region is

    (A) $1 - \frac{\pi}{4}$ (B) $1 - \frac{\pi}{2}$

    (C) $\frac{\pi}{4} - 1$ (D) $1 + \frac{\pi}{4}$

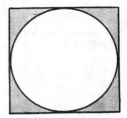

38. If p is one angle of a regular pentagon and d is one angle of a regular decagon, then $\frac{p}{d} =$

    (A) $\frac{1}{2}$ (B) $\frac{2}{3}$ (C) $\frac{3}{4}$ (D) $\frac{2}{1}$

39. If the edges of a cube are each doubled, what is the percent of increase in the volume?

    (A) 200   (B) 400   (C) 600   (D) 700

40. Point O is the common center for the half-circle with radius $\overline{OB}$ and for the half-circle with radius $\overline{OA}$. A, B, O, C, and D all lie on the same straight line. B and C are the midpoints of $\overline{OA}$ and $\overline{OD}$ respectively. What is the difference between the degree measures of $\overparen{BC}$ and $\overparen{AD}$?

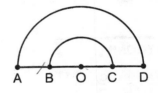

    (A) 0   (B) 45

    (C) 90   (D) 180

Answer Sheet

Diagnostic Test 2

ANGLES

1. Ⓐ Ⓑ Ⓒ Ⓓ
2. Ⓐ Ⓑ Ⓒ Ⓓ
3. Ⓐ Ⓑ Ⓒ Ⓓ
4. Ⓐ Ⓑ Ⓒ Ⓓ

LINES

5. Ⓐ Ⓑ Ⓒ Ⓓ
6. Ⓐ Ⓑ Ⓒ Ⓓ
7. Ⓐ Ⓑ Ⓒ Ⓓ
8. Ⓐ Ⓑ Ⓒ Ⓓ

POLYGONS

9. Ⓐ Ⓑ Ⓒ Ⓓ
10. Ⓐ Ⓑ Ⓒ Ⓓ
11. Ⓐ Ⓑ Ⓒ Ⓓ
12. Ⓐ Ⓑ Ⓒ Ⓓ

TRIANGLES

13. Ⓐ Ⓑ Ⓒ Ⓓ
14. Ⓐ Ⓑ Ⓒ Ⓓ
15. Ⓐ Ⓑ Ⓒ Ⓓ
16. Ⓐ Ⓑ Ⓒ Ⓓ

CIRCLES

17. Ⓐ Ⓑ Ⓒ Ⓓ
18. Ⓐ Ⓑ Ⓒ Ⓓ
19. Ⓐ Ⓑ Ⓒ Ⓓ
20. Ⓐ Ⓑ Ⓒ Ⓓ

PERIMETER

21. Ⓐ Ⓑ Ⓒ Ⓓ
22. Ⓐ Ⓑ Ⓒ Ⓓ
23. Ⓐ Ⓑ Ⓒ Ⓓ
24. Ⓐ Ⓑ Ⓒ Ⓓ

AREA

25. Ⓐ Ⓑ Ⓒ Ⓓ
26. Ⓐ Ⓑ Ⓒ Ⓓ
27. Ⓐ Ⓑ Ⓒ Ⓓ
28. Ⓐ Ⓑ Ⓒ Ⓓ

VOLUME

29. Ⓐ Ⓑ Ⓒ Ⓓ
30. Ⓐ Ⓑ Ⓒ Ⓓ
31. Ⓐ Ⓑ Ⓒ Ⓓ
32. Ⓐ Ⓑ Ⓒ Ⓓ

COORDINATE GEOMETRY

33. Ⓐ Ⓑ Ⓒ Ⓓ
34. Ⓐ Ⓑ Ⓒ Ⓓ
35. Ⓐ Ⓑ Ⓒ Ⓓ
36. Ⓐ Ⓑ Ⓒ Ⓓ

PROBLEM SOLVING

37. Ⓐ Ⓑ Ⓒ Ⓓ
38. Ⓐ Ⓑ Ⓒ Ⓓ
39. Ⓐ Ⓑ Ⓒ Ⓓ
40. Ⓐ Ⓑ Ⓒ Ⓓ

Diagnostic Test 2

Directions:
Solve each problem in this Diagnostic Test. Use any available space on the page for scratchwork. Then decide which is the best of the choices given and either darken the corresponding space on the Answer Sheet on page 16 or circle your answer from among the choices provided.

ANGLES

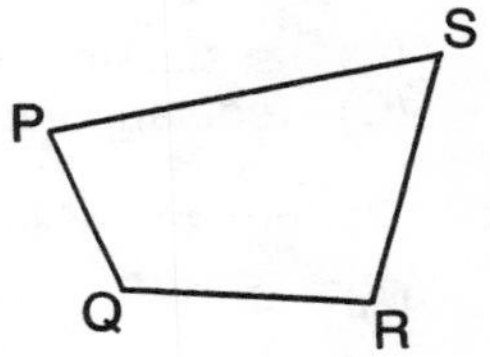

1. In the figure at the right, what is the vertex of $\angle$ PQR?

(A) P   (B) Q
(C) R   (D) S

2. If two angles are supplementary, then the sum of their degree measures is

(A) 60   (B) 90   (C) 180   (D) 360

Questions 3-4 refer to the diagram at the right.

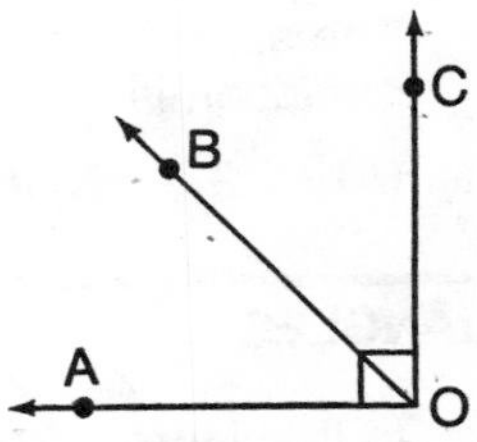

3. If $\overrightarrow{OB}$ bisects $\angle$ AOC, then the degree measure of $\angle$ BOC is

(A) 30   (B) 45
(C) 60   (D) 90

4. $\angle$ AOB and $\angle$ BOC are

(A) vertical angles   (B) obtuse angles
(C) adjacent angles   (D) right angles

LINES

5. In how many points do two distinct parallel lines intersect?

(A) 0   (B) 1   (C) 2   (D) 3

Questions 6-8 refer to the diagram at the right.

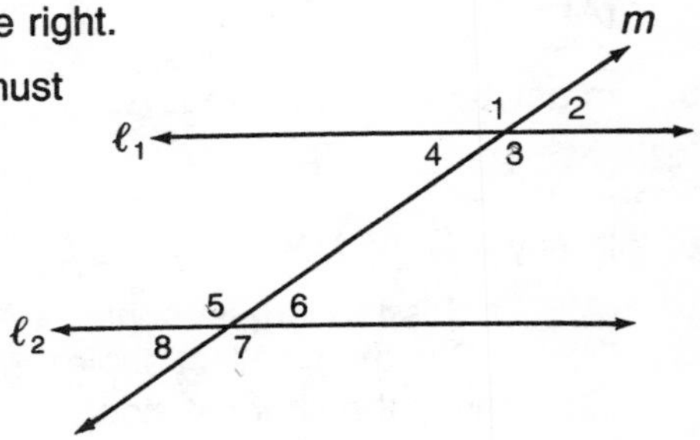

6. If $\ell_1 \parallel \ell_2$, which of the following must be true?

(A) $\angle 1 \cong \angle 2$
(B) $\angle 2 \cong \angle 7$
(C) $\angle 5 \cong \angle 2$
(D) $\angle 4 \cong \angle 6$

7. ∠ 1 and ∠ 5 are

(A)   vertical angles   (B)   corresponding angles
(C)   base angles   (D)   alternate interior angles

8. If m ∠ 1 = 120°, then m ∠ 7 =

(A)   60°   (B)   90°   (C)   100°   (D)   120°

POLYGONS

9. If 4 sides of a quadrilateral are congruent, then the quadrilateral is

(A)   a square   (B)   a rhombus
(C)   equiangular   (D)   a regular polygon

10. The number of sides an octagon has is

(A)   4   (B)   5   (C)   6   (D)   8

11. If two polygons have the same shape, they must be

(A)   similar   (B)   congruent
(C)   regular   (D)   equilateral

12. The sum of the degree measures of all the exterior angles of a pentagon is

(A)   72   (B)   180   (C)   360   (D)   540

TRIANGLES

13. In the figure at the right, if $\overline{AD} \perp \overline{BC}$, then $\overline{AD}$ is a(n)

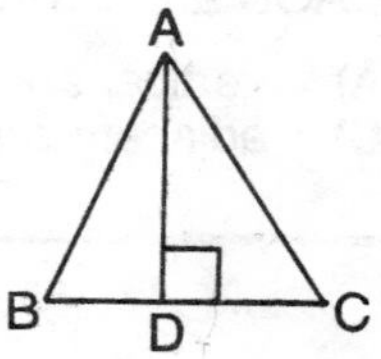

(A)   bisector   (B)   median
(C)   hypotenuse   (D)   altitude

14. In right triangle XYZ with right angle Y, if XZ = 25 and YZ = 24, then XY =

(A)   1   (B)   7   (C)   49   (D) $\sqrt{1201}$

15. In any triangle ABC, m ∠ A + m ∠ B + m ∠ C =

(A)   90°   (B)   120°   (C)   180°   (D)   360°

16. In any triangle MNP, if $\overline{MP}$ is the longest side, then

(A)   ∠ N is the largest angle
(B)   ∠ P is the smallest angle
(C) $\overline{MN}$ is the shortest side
(D)   ∠ M > ∠ P

CIRCLES

Questions 17-20 refer to the diagram at the right.

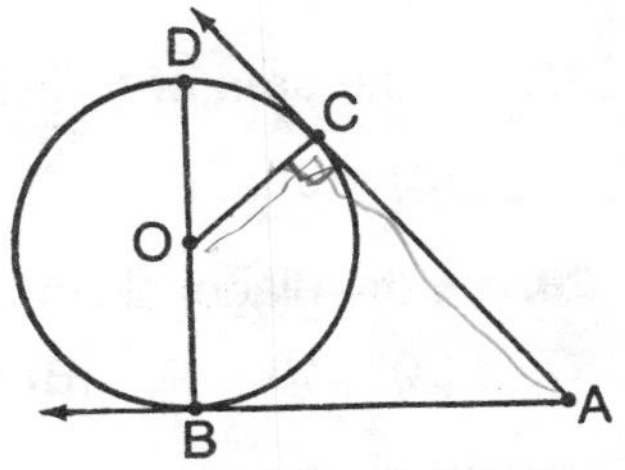

17. Which line segments are congruent?

    (A) $\overline{AC}$ and $\overline{AB}$
    (B) $\overline{BD}$ and $\overline{AB}$
    (C) $\overline{AC}$ and $\overline{BD}$
    (D) $\overline{OC}$ and $\overline{BD}$

18. Which line segment is a diameter?

    (A) OD   (B) BD   (C) OC   (D) AB

19. The m $\angle$ OCA =

    (A) 30°   (B) 45°   (C) 60°   (D) 90°

20. If m $\overset{\frown}{BC}$ = 130°, then m $\angle$ A =

    (A) 30°   (B) 50°   (C) 90°   (D) 130°

PERIMETER

21. If each side of a square is a, the perimeter is

    (A) 2a (B) 3a (C) 4a (D) a^2

22. If the three sides of a triangle are 7, $x + 3$, and $2x - 3$, and if the perimeter is 28, then x =

    (A) 5   (B) 7   (C) 9   (D) $9\frac{1}{3}$

23. If two adjacent sides of a parallelogram have length 6 and 10, then the perimeter is

    (A) 16   (B) 22   (C) 26   (D) 32

24. If the perimeter of a regular decagon is 48, the length of a side is

    (A) 4.8   (B) 6   (C) 8   (D) 9.6

AREA

25. If the base and altitude of a triangle are 9 and 12 respectively, the area of the triangle is

    (A) 27   (B) 49   (C) 54   (D) 108

26. If the ratio of the length to the width of a rectangle is 3 : 1 and the area is 48, then the width is

(A) 4   (B) 8   (C) 12   (D) 16

27. If the area of a circle is π, then the diameter is

(A) 0   (B) $\frac{1}{2}$ (C) 1   (D) 2

28. If the diagonals of a rhombus are 4 and 10, then the area is

(A) 10   (B) 20   (C) 30   (D) 40

VOLUME

29. If the volume of a cube is $64a^3$, then the edge of the cube is

(A) $2a$ (B) $4a$ (C) $4a^2$ (D) $8a$

30. If the dimensions of a rectangular prism are 4 by 2 by 3, then the volume is

(A) 9   (B) 24   (C) 48   (D) 58

31. If the volume of a prism is 30 and the area of its base is 6, then the height is

(A) 5   (B) 24   (C) 36   (D) 180

32. The volume V of a pyramid is $V = \frac{1}{3}Bh$, where B is the area of the base and h is the height. If $B = 6$ and $h = 9$, then $V =$

(A) 6   (B) 18   (C) 21   (D) 54

COORDINATE GEOMETRY

33. The endpoints of a diameter of a circle are $(-3, -2)$ and $(11, -10)$. The coordinates of the center of the circle are

(A) $(2, -3)$ (B) $(4, -6)$

(C) $(8, -12)$ (D) $(-7, -6)$

34. In $\triangle ABC$, the coordinates of A are $(2, 4)$ and the coordinates of B are $(-1, 3)$. The length of $\overline{AB}$ is

(A) $\sqrt{10}$ (B) 5

(C) $\sqrt{7}$ (D) 10

35. The coordinates of the vertices of parallelogram ABCD are A(0, 0), B(4, 0), C(7, 1), and D(x, 1). The numerical value of x is

(A) 1   (B) 2   (C) 3   (D) 4

36. The area of parallelogram ABCD whose vertices have the coordinates A(0, 0), B(4, 0), C(5, 4), and D(1, 4) is

(A) 4   (B) 8   (C) 16   (D) 20

PROBLEM SOLVING

37. The interior angle of a regular hexagon is represented by a. The exterior angle of a regular octagon is represented by b. The ratio of a to b is

(A) 3 : 8   (B) 4 : 3
(C) 2 : 1   (D) 8 : 3

38. If the area of a circle is equal to the area of the triangle shown at the right, the radius of the circle is

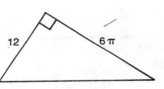

(A) 2   (B) 3
(C) 3π (D) 6

39. In the figure at the right, if a side of the larger square is x, then the area of the smaller square is

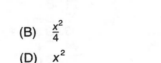

(A) $\frac{x^2}{2}$ (B) $\frac{x^2}{4}$

(C) $\frac{3}{4}x^2$ (D) x^2

40. In isosceles triangle MNP, $\overline{MN} \cong \overline{NP}$, and $\overline{NQ}$ is the altitude to the base $\overline{MP}$. If NQ = y, NP = $2y - 3$, and MP = $2y - 2$, then the length of $\overline{NQ}$ is

(A) 1   (B) 2   (C) 3   (D) 4

Answer Key to Diagnostic Tests

Following each answer, there is a number or numbers in the form "*a.b*" in parentheses. This number refers to the Geometry Refresher Sections (beginning on page 23). The first number "*a*" indicates the section:

1. Angles	6. Perimeter
2. Lines	7. Area
3. Polygons	8. Volume
4. Triangles	9. Coordinate Geometry
5. Circles	10. Problem Solving

The number "*b*" indicates the part of the section that explains the rule or method used in solving the problem.

DIAGNOSTIC TEST 1

1. D (1.9)	**15.** D (4.3)	**29.** D (8.1)
2. B (1.7)	**16.** C (4.2)	**30.** B (8.1)
3. B (1.5, 1.4)	**17.** C (5.1)	**31.** D (8.1)
4. D (1.4)	**18.** D (5.4)	**32.** D (8.2)
5. B (2.1)	**19.** C (5.4)	**33.** A (9.5, 9.4)
6. C (2.6)	**20.** A (5.8)	**34.** B (9.5)
7. B (2.4, 2.1)	**21.** B (6.3)	**35.** D (9.7)
8. A (2.8)	**22.** B (6.2)	**36.** C (9.5)
9. B (3.4)	**23.** C (6.1, 3.2)	**37.** A (10.7, 7.1, 7.6)
10. C (3.2)	**24.** D (6.3)	**38.** C (10.3, 3.2)
11. D (3.6)	**25.** B (7.5)	**39.** D (8.1)
12. B (3.3, 3.2)	**26.** C (7.6, 5.1)	**40.** A (5.6, 5.5)
13. A (4.5)	**27.** D (7.1)	
14. B (4.3, 4.5)	**28.** A (7.1)	

DIAGNOSTIC TEST 2

1. B (1.1)	**15.** C (4.3)	**29.** B (8.1)
2. C (1.8)	**16.** A (4.7)	**30.** B (8.1)
3. B (1.4, 1.5)	**17.** A (5.4)	**31.** A (8.1)
4. C (1.6)	**18.** B (5.1)	**32.** B (8.2)
5. A (2.5)	**19.** D (5.4)	**33.** B (9.9, 5.1)
6. D (2.6)	**20.** B (5.8, 5.5)	**34.** A (9.7)
7. B (2.6)	**21.** C (6.3)	**35.** C (9.7, 9.6, 9.5)
8. D (1.9, 2.6)	**22.** B (6.2)	**36.** C (9.6, 9.5, 7.2)
9. B (3.6)	**23.** D (6.1, 3.6)	**37.** D (10.3, 3.3, 3.2)
10. D (3.2)	**24.** A (6.1, 3.2)	**38.** D (7.5, 7.6)
11. A (3.5)	**25.** C (7.5)	**39.** A (10.7, 7.1)
12. C (3.3, 3.2)	**26.** A (7.1)	**40.** D (4.8, 4.2, 4.5)
13. D (4.2)	**27.** D (7.6, 5.1)	
14. B (4.8)	**28.** B (7.3)	

Part Two

Geometry Refresher Sections

The Geometry Refresher Sections provide a carefully developed review of concepts and skills in geometry. These sections contain definitions, illustrations, and examples designed to help you solve many different types of geometry questions which appear on actual standardized tests in mathematics. Be sure you are familiar with and understand each of the illustrated methods and examples.

Geometry Refresher

Angles, Lines, Polygons, Triangles, Circles, Perimeter, Area, Volume, Coordinate Geometry, and Problem Solving

---

ANGLES

An *angle* is formed by two distinct rays with a common endpoint.

1.1 Reading and Naming an Angle

The two *rays* are called the *sides* of the angle and their common endpoint is the *vertex* of the angle. The symbol $\angle$ is used to indicate an angle. The symbol $\longrightarrow$ is used to indicate a ray. In the diagram below, $\overrightarrow{BA}$ and $\overrightarrow{BC}$ are rays and B is the vertex. The angle may be designated by

1. the name of the endpoint and a point on each of the rays forming the angle with the vertex letter written in the center ($\angle$ ABC or $\angle$ CBA).
2. its vertex ($\angle$ B).
3. the letter indicated inside the angle ($\angle b$).

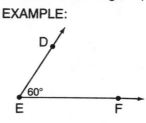

1.2 Measure of an Angle

The *measure of an angle* is the amount of rotation of a ray from its initial position to a terminating position. The unit of measure is the degree (°).

EXAMPLE:

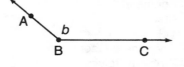

The measure of $\angle$ DEF is 60° or m $\angle$ DEF = 60°.

1.3 Congruent Angles

Angles with the same measure are called *congruent angles*.

EXAMPLE:
If m $\angle x$ = 72° and m $\angle y$ = 72°, then $\angle x \cong \angle y$, which is read as "$\angle x$ is congruent to $\angle y$."

EXAMPLE:
∠ ABC ≅ ∠ DEF and m ∠ ABC = m ∠ DEF are equivalent
statements.

1.4 Angle Bisector

An *angle bisector* is the ray that divides an angle into two
congruent angles.

EXAMPLE:

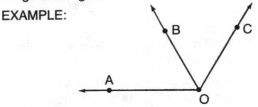

$\overrightarrow{OB}$ is the angle bisector of ∠ AOC, so ∠ AOB ≅ ∠ BOC or
m ∠ AOB = m ∠ BOC.

1.5 Classifying Angles

Angles are classified by their measures.

EXAMPLES:

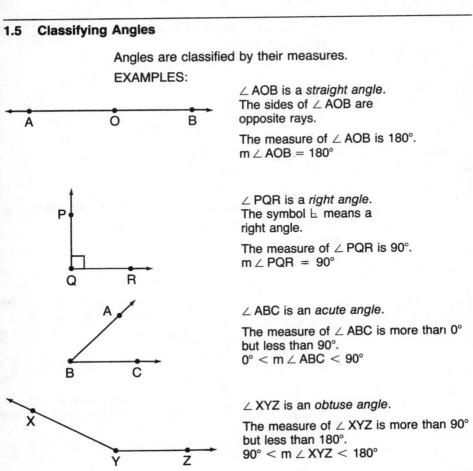

∠ AOB is a *straight angle*.
The sides of ∠ AOB are
opposite rays.

The measure of ∠ AOB is 180°.
m ∠ AOB = 180°

∠ PQR is a *right angle*.
The symbol ∟ means a
right angle.

The measure of ∠ PQR is 90°.
m ∠ PQR = 90°

∠ ABC is an *acute angle*.

The measure of ∠ ABC is more than 0°
but less than 90°.
0° < m ∠ ABC < 90°

∠ XYZ is an *obtuse angle*.

The measure of ∠ XYZ is more than 90°
but less than 180°.
90° < m ∠ XYZ < 180°

1.6 Adjacent Angles

Adjacent angles are two angles having the same vertex and a common side.

EXAMPLE:

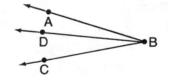

∠ ABD and ∠ DBC are adjacent angles with vertex B and common side $\overrightarrow{BD}$.

∠ ABC and ∠ DBC share the common vertex B and the common side $\overrightarrow{BC}$ but are *not* adjacent angles because, to be adjacent, one angle may not be inside the other.

1.7 Complementary Angles

Two angles are *complementary* when the sum of their degree measures is 90.

EXAMPLE:

If m ∠ 3 + m ∠ 4 = 90°, then ∠ 3 is the complement of ∠ 4, and ∠ 4 is the complement of ∠ 3.

Angles complementary to the same or congruent angles are congruent.

EXAMPLE:

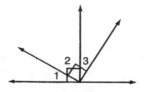

∠ 1 is the complement of ∠ 2, and ∠ 3 is the complement of ∠ 2.

Thus, ∠ 1 ≅ ∠ 3.

EXAMPLE:

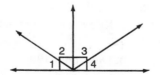

∠ 1 is the complement of ∠ 2, ∠ 3 is the complement of ∠ 4, and ∠ 2 ≅ ∠ 3.

Thus, ∠ 1 ≅ ∠ 4.

1.8 Supplementary Angles

Two angles are *supplementary* when the sum of their degree measures is 180.

EXAMPLE:

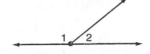

If m ∠ 1 + m ∠ 2 = 180°, then ∠ 1 is the supplement of ∠ 2 and ∠ 2 is the supplement of ∠ 1.

Angles supplementary to the same or congruent angles are congruent.

EXAMPLE:

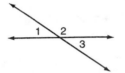

∠ 1 is the supplement of ∠ 2, and ∠ 3 is the supplement of ∠ 2.

Thus, ∠ 1 ≅ ∠ 3.

EXAMPLE:

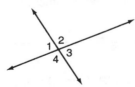

∠ 1 is the supplement of ∠ 2, ∠ 3 is the supplement of ∠ 4, and ∠ 1 ≅ ∠ 3.

Thus, ∠ 2 ≅ ∠ 4.

1.9 Vertical Angles

When two lines meet, they form four angles. The opposite angles are called *vertical angles*.

EXAMPLE:

∠ 1 and ∠ 3 are vertical angles.
∠ 2 and ∠ 4 are vertical angles.

The two angles in a pair of vertical angles are congruent. Thus, ∠ 1 ≅ ∠ 3 and ∠ 2 ≅ ∠ 4.

LINES

A *line* is a collection of an infinite number of points. A line has no width.

2.1 Lines and Line Segments

- **Line**

  A line extends without end in two opposite directions.

  EXAMPLE:

  $\overrightarrow{AB}$ or $\overrightarrow{BA}$ may be used to identify the line.
  The lower case letter ℓ names the same line.

  - Every straight line contains at least two distinct points and two points determine a line.
  - The intersection of two distinct straight lines is a point.

- **Line Segment**

  A *line segment* is part of a line with two endpoints.

  EXAMPLE:

  The segment is named by the symbol $\overline{DE}$ or $\overline{ED}$.

2.2 Congruent Line Segments

Segments with the same measure, or length, are called *congruent segments*.

EXAMPLE:
If AB = 8 in. and CD = 8 in., then $\overline{AB} \cong \overline{CD}$.

2.3 Midpoints

A point is the *midpoint* of a line segment if it divides the line segment into two congruent segments.

EXAMPLE:

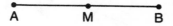

If $\overline{AM} \cong \overline{MB}$ or AM = MB, then M is the midpoint of $\overline{AB}$.

The midpoint of a line segment bisects the segment; that is, it divides the segment into two congruent segments.

EXAMPLE:
If M is the midpoint of $\overline{AB}$, then $\overline{AM} \cong \overline{MB}$ or AM = MB.

2.4 Perpendicular Lines

If two lines are *perpendicular*, they meet at right angles.

EXAMPLE:

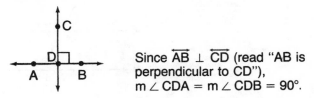

Since $\overleftrightarrow{AB} \perp \overleftrightarrow{CD}$ (read "AB is perpendicular to CD"), $m \angle CDA = m \angle CDB = 90°$.

If two lines meet at right angles, they are perpendicular. Since $\angle CDB$ is a right angle, $\overleftrightarrow{AB} \perp \overleftrightarrow{CD}$.

2.5 Parallel Lines

Two lines are *parallel* if they lie in the same plane and do not intersect.

EXAMPLE:

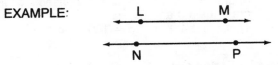

$\overleftrightarrow{LM}$ and $\overleftrightarrow{NP}$ represent parallel lines.
This is indicated by writing $\overleftrightarrow{LM} \parallel \overleftrightarrow{NP}$.

Two parallel lines are everywhere equidistant.

EXAMPLE:

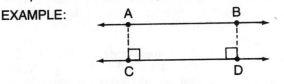

If $\overleftrightarrow{AB} \parallel \overleftrightarrow{CD}$, $\overline{AC} \perp \overleftrightarrow{CD}$, and $\overline{BD} \perp \overleftrightarrow{CD}$, then $\overline{AC} \cong \overline{BD}$ or AC = BD.

2.6 Transversals and Special Angles

A line that intersects two or more lines is a *transversal*.

EXAMPLE:

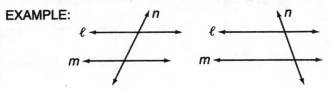

Line $\ell \parallel$ line m, and line n is a transversal.

If two parallel lines are cut by a transversal, then
1. the *alternate interior angles* are congruent.
2. the *corresponding angles* are congruent.
3. the *consecutive interior angles* are supplementary.

EXAMPLE:

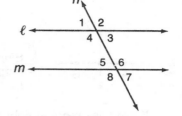

Angles 4 and 6 are alternate interior angles as are angles 3 and 5.
Thus, $\angle 4 \cong \angle 6$, and $\angle 3 \cong \angle 5$.

Pairs of corresponding angles are angles 1 and 5, 2 and 6, 4 and 8, and 3 and 7.
Thus, $\angle 1 \cong \angle 5$, $\angle 2 \cong \angle 6$, $\angle 4 \cong \angle 8$, and $\angle 3 \cong \angle 7$.

Angles 4 and 5 are a pair of consecutive interior angles as are angles 3 and 6.
Thus, $m \angle 4 + m \angle 5 = 180°$ and $m \angle 3 + m \angle 6 = 180°$.

2.7 Converse of a Statement

If the antecedent and the consequent are interchanged, then the *converse* of the statement is formed. Remember that the converse is not always true even if the original statement is true.

These are the converses of the parallel lines theorems:
If two lines in the same plane are cut by a transversal so that
1. the corresponding angles are congruent, or
2. the alternate interior angles are congruent, or
3. the consecutive interior angles are supplementary,
then the lines are parallel.

2.8 Parallel and Perpendicular Lines

If two lines are perpendicular to the same line, the two lines are parallel to each other.

EXAMPLE:

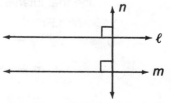

If line $\ell \perp$ line n and line $m \perp$ line n, then line $\ell \parallel$ line m.

If two lines are parallel to the same line, the two lines are parallel to each other.

EXAMPLE:

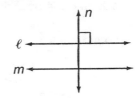

If line ℓ ∥ line n and line m ∥ line n, then line ℓ ∥ line m.

If a line is perpendicular to one of two parallel lines, it is pependicular to the other line.

EXAMPLE:

If line ℓ ∥ line m and line n ⊥ line ℓ, then line n ⊥ line m.

POLYGONS

A *polygon* is a simple closed curve formed by line segments called the sides of the polygon.

3.1 Characteristics

The sides of a polygon intersect exactly two other sides only at their endpoints called the vertices (plural of "vertex"). A polygon is referred to by giving its vertices in the order in which they are joined.

EXAMPLES:

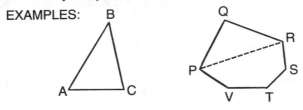

Polygon ABC   Polygon PQRSTV

Line segment PR is a *diagonal* of the polygon PQRSTV, since it connects two nonconsecutive vertices of the polygon.

- A polygon with all sides congruent is *equilateral*.

- A polygon with all angles congruent is *equiangular*.

- A *regular polygon* is a polygon that is both equilateral and equiangular.

31

EXAMPLE:

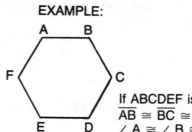

If ABCDEF is a regular polygon, then $\overline{AB} \cong \overline{BC} \cong \overline{CD} \cong \overline{DE} \cong \overline{EF} \cong \overline{FA}$ and $\angle A \cong \angle B \cong \angle C \cong \angle D \cong \angle E \cong \angle F$.

An *exterior angle* of a polygon is an angle formed by one side and the opposite ray of an adjacent side of the polygon

EXAMPLES:

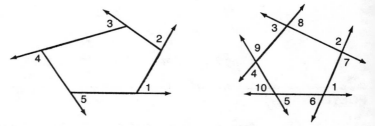

One exterior angle at each vertex is shown in the polygon on the left. Each of the 10 exterior angles is shown in the polygon on the right.

3.2 Naming Polygons

Polygons are named by the number of sides forming them.

Number of Sides	Name
3	*tri*angle
4	*quadri*lateral
5	*penta*gon
6	*hexa*gon
8	*octa*gon
10	*deca*gon

3.3 Measures of the Angles of a Polygon

- The sum of the measures of the angles of a polygon of n sides is $(n - 2)180°$.

EXAMPLE: What is the sum of the measures of the angles of a pentagon?

A pentagon has 5 sides, so substitute 5 for n.
Therefore, $(5 - 2)180° = (3)180° = 540°$

- The measure of one angle of a regular polygon of n sides is $\frac{(n-2)180°}{n}$.

  EXAMPLE: What is the measure of one angle of a regular pentagon?

  Substitute 5 for n.
  Therefore, $\frac{(5-2)180°}{5} = \frac{3(180°)}{5} = 108°$.

- The sum of the measures of the exterior angles of a polygon, one at each vertex, is always 360° no matter how many sides the polygon has.

  EXAMPLE: Four of the exterior angles of a hexagon measure 35°, 60°, 75°, and 50°. The other angles are congruent to each other. Find their measure.

  Let x = degree measure of each of the congruent angles.

  Then, $\quad 35 + 60 + 75 + 50 + x + x = 360$
  $$2x + 220 = 360$$
  $$2x = 140$$
  $$x = 70$$

  The measure of each of the congruent angles is 70°.

- The measure of each exterior angle of a regular polygon of n sides is $\frac{360°}{n}$.

  EXAMPLE: How many sides has a regular polygon if the measure of each exterior angle is 40°?

  $$\frac{360°}{n} = 40°$$
  $$40n = 360$$
  $$n = 9$$

3.4 Congruent Polygons

Congruent polygons are polygons whose corresponding sides are congruent and whose corresponding angles are congruent.

EXAMPLE:

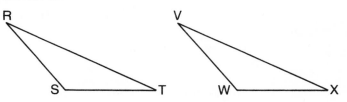

If $\triangle RST \cong \triangle VWX$, then $\overline{RS} \cong \overline{VW}$, $\overline{ST} \cong \overline{WX}$, $\overline{RT} \cong \overline{VX}$, $\angle R \cong \angle V$, $\angle S \cong \angle W$, and $\angle T \cong \angle X$.

3.5   Similar Polygons

Similar polygons are polygons that have their corresponding angles congruent and the measures of their corresponding sides proportional. The symbol "~" is read as "is similar to."

EXAMPLE:

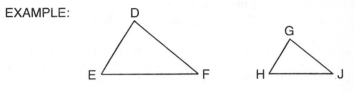

If $\triangle$ DEF ~ $\triangle$ GHJ, then $\angle$ D $\cong$ $\angle$ G, $\angle$ E $\cong$ $\angle$ H, $\angle$ F $\cong$ $\angle$ J, and $\frac{DE}{GH} = \frac{EF}{HJ} = \frac{DF}{GJ}$.

3.6   Quadrilaterals

● **Parallelogram**
A *parallelogram* is a quadrilateral whose opposite sides are parallel.

EXAMPLE:

ABCD is a parallelogram, so $\overline{AB}$ ∥ $\overline{DC}$ and $\overline{AD}$ ∥ $\overline{BC}$.

$\overline{DE}$ is an *altitude* of parallelogram ABCD. The measure of an altitude is called the *height*.

● **Properties of a Parallelogram**
  • The pairs of opposite sides are congruent.
  • The pairs of opposite angles are congruent.
  • Two consecutive angles are supplementary.
  • The diagonals bisect each other.

EXAMPLE:

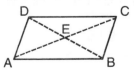

ABCD is a parallelogram, so
  • $\overline{AB} \cong \overline{DC}$ and $\overline{AD} \cong \overline{BC}$
  • $\angle$ A $\cong$ $\angle$ C and $\angle$ B $\cong$ $\angle$ D
  • m$\angle$ A + m$\angle$ D $= 180°$
    m$\angle$ D + m$\angle$ C $= 180°$
    m$\angle$ C + m$\angle$ B $= 180°$
    m$\angle$ B + m$\angle$ A $= 180°$
  • $\overline{DE} \cong \overline{EB}$ and $\overline{AE} \cong \overline{EC}$

- **Rectangle**
  A *rectangle* is a parallelogram with four right angles.

  EXAMPLE:

  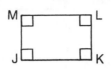

  JKLM is a rectangle, so $m\angle J = m\angle K = m\angle L = m\angle M = 90°$.

  The diagonals are congruent.

  EXAMPLE:

  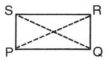

  PQRS is a rectangle, so $\overline{PR} \cong \overline{QS}$.

- **Rhombus**
  A *rhombus* is a parallelogram with all sides congruent.

  EXAMPLE:

  WXYZ is a rhombus, so $\overline{WX} \cong \overline{XY} \cong \overline{YZ} \cong \overline{ZW}$.

  The diagonals of a rhombus are perpendicular to each other and bisect the angles.

  EXAMPLE:

  ABCD is a rhombus, so $\overline{AC} \perp \overline{BD}$, $\overline{AC}$ bisects $\angle A$ and $\angle C$, and $\overline{BD}$ bisects $\angle B$ and $\angle D$.

- **Square**
  A *square* is a rectangle with two congruent adjacent sides.

  EXAMPLE:

  WXYZ is a square, so $\overline{WX} \cong \overline{XY} \cong \overline{YZ} \cong \overline{ZW}$.

- **Trapezoid**
  A *trapezoid* is a quadrilateral having only one pair of parallel sides called the *bases*.

  EXAMPLE:

  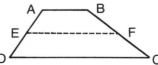

  ABCD is a trapezoid with bases $\overline{AB}$ and $\overline{DC}$ parallel to each other. $\overline{AD}$ and $\overline{BC}$ are the *legs* and $\overline{EF}$ is the *median* joining E and F, the midpoints of the legs.

An isosceles trapezoid has congruent legs.

EXAMPLE:

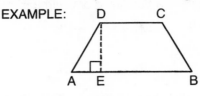

ABCD is an isosceles trapezoid, so $\overline{AD} \cong \overline{BC}$. $\overline{DE}$ is an altitude.

TRIANGLES

A *triangle* is a polygon that has three sides.

4.1 Classifying Triangles

Triangles may be classified by the measures of their angles or by the lengths of their sides.

EXAMPLES:

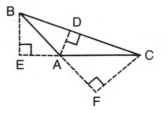

Equilateral Triangle (all sides congruent)

Isosceles Triangle (at least 2 sides congruent)

Right Triangle (1 right angle)

4.2 Auxiliary Lines in a Triangle

1. An altitude in a triangle is a segment drawn from a vertex perpendicular to the opposite side.

2. A median in a triangle is a segment drawn from a vertex to the midpoint of the opposite side.

3. An angle bisector is a segment drawn from a vertex bisecting the angle and ending on the opposite side.

EXAMPLES:

Altitudes: $\overline{AD}$, $\overline{BE}$, and $\overline{CF}$

$m\angle\,ADC = m\angle\,BEA = m\angle\,CFA = 90°$

Medians: $\overline{RD}$, $\overline{TS}$, and $\overline{BC}$

$\overline{TD} \cong \overline{DB}$, $\overline{RC} \cong \overline{CT}$, and $\overline{RS} \cong \overline{SB}$

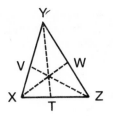

Angle bisectors: $\overline{XW}$, $\overline{ZV}$, and $\overline{YT}$

$\angle\,YXW \cong \angle\,ZXW$
$\angle\,XZV \cong \angle\,YZV$
$\angle\,XYT \cong \angle\,ZYT$

4.3 Angle Measure

The sum of the measures of the angles of a triangle is 180°.

EXAMPLE:

ABC is a triangle, so $a + b + c = 180$.

Each angle in an equilateral triangle is 60°.

EXAMPLE:

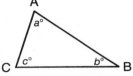

In $\triangle$ ABC, $\overline{AB} \cong \overline{BC} \cong \overline{CA}$, so $a = b = c = 60$.

4.4 Congruent Triangles

Congruent triangles are triangles whose corresponding sides are congruent and whose corresponding angles are congruent.

Figures can be marked, as shown below, to indicate congruent sides and angles. If $\overline{AB} \cong \overline{DE}$, then both $\overline{AB}$ and $\overline{DE}$ are given one mark. If $\overline{BC} \cong \overline{EF}$, then both $\overline{BC}$ and $\overline{EF}$ are given two marks. Angles are marked in the same way.

Case I: If three sides of one triangle are congruent to three sides of another triangle, the triangles are congruent. (SSS)

EXAMPLE:

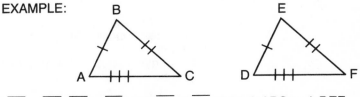

If $\overline{AB} \cong \overline{DE}$, $\overline{BC} \cong \overline{EF}$, and $\overline{AC} \cong \overline{DF}$, then $\triangle$ ABC $\cong$ $\triangle$ DEF.

Case II: If two sides and the included angle of one triangle are congruent to two sides and the included angle of another triangle, the triangles are congruent. (SAS)

EXAMPLE:

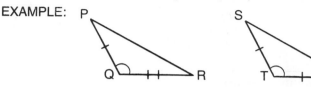

If $\overline{PQ} \cong \overline{ST}$, $\overline{QR} \cong \overline{TV}$, and $\angle Q \cong \angle T$, then $\triangle PQR \cong \triangle STV$.

Case III: If two angles and the included side of one triangle are congruent to two angles and the included side of another triangle, the triangles are congruent. (ASA)

EXAMPLE:

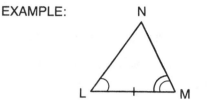

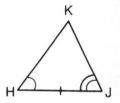

If $\angle L \cong \angle H$, $\angle M \cong \angle J$, and $\overline{LM} \cong \overline{HJ}$, then $\triangle LMN \cong \triangle HJK$.

Case IV: If two angles and a side opposite one of the angles in one triangle are congruent to two angles and a side opposite the corresponding angle in the other triangle, then the triangles are congruent. (SAA)

EXAMPLE:

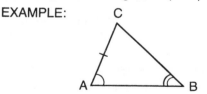

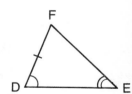

If $\angle A \cong \angle D$, $\angle B \cong \angle E$, and $\overline{AC} \cong \overline{DF}$, then $\triangle ABC \cong \triangle DEF$.

4.5 Isosceles Triangles

In an isosceles triangle
1. the sides opposite the congruent angles are congruent.
2. the angles opposite the congruent sides are congruent.

EXAMPLE: Triangle DEF is isosceles.

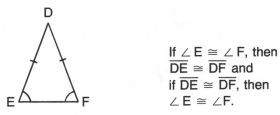

If ∠ E ≅ ∠ F, then
$\overline{DE}$ ≅ $\overline{DF}$ and
if $\overline{DE}$ ≅ $\overline{DF}$, then
∠ E ≅ ∠F.

The bisector of the vertex angle (the angle formed by the congruent sides) of an isosceles triangle bisects the base and is perpendicular to it.

EXAMPLE: Triangle ABC is isosceles.

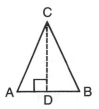

If $\overline{CD}$ bisects ∠ C, then
$\overline{AD}$ ≅ $\overline{DB}$ and $\overline{CD}$ ⊥ $\overline{AB}$.

4.6   Exterior Angle of a Triangle

The measure of an exterior angle of a triangle is equal to the sum of the measures of the nonadjacent angles of the triangle.

EXAMPLE:

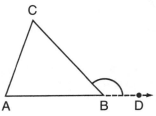

∠ CBD is an exterior angle
of △ ABC, so
m ∠ CBD = m∠ A + m∠ C.

Recall the following symbols:
> means "is greater than."
< means "is less than."

The measure of an exterior angle of a triangle is greater than the measures of either of the nonadjacent angles of the triangle.

EXAMPLE: In the figure above, m ∠ CBD > m ∠ A and
m ∠ CBD > m∠ C.

4.7 Inequalities in a Triangle

Two inequalities are of the *same order* if, in each case, the symbols point in the same direction, and are of the *opposite order* if they do not.

EXAMPLES:

	Same Order	Opposite Order
	If 4 > 1, then 3 > 0.	If 10 > 5,
	If 4 < 6, then 1 < 3.	then $-2 < -1$.

- If the measures of two sides of a triangle are unequal, the measures of the angles opposite these sides are unequal in the same order.

EXAMPLE:

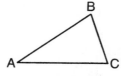

In △ABC, if AB > BC, then m∠C > m∠A.

- If the measures of two angles of a triangle are unequal, the measures of the sides opposite these angles are unequal in the same order.

EXAMPLE: In △ABC, if m∠B > m∠A, then AC > BC.

- The sum of the measures of two sides of a triangle is greater than the measure of the third side.

EXAMPLE: In △ABC, AB + BC > AC, AB + AC > BC, and BC + AC > AB.

4.8 Right Triangles

In a right triangle, the side opposite the right angle is called the *hypotenuse* and the other two sides are called the *legs*.

EXAMPLE:

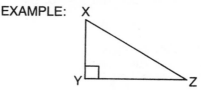

Hypotenuse $\overline{XZ}$
Legs $\overline{XY}$ and $\overline{YZ}$

- **Pythagorean Theorem**
The square of the measure of the hypotenuse of a right triangle is equal to the sum of the squares of the measures of the legs.

EXAMPLE: In triangle XYZ above, $(XY)^2 + (YZ)^2 = (XZ)^2$.

- **30-60-90 Triangles**
  The special properties of these right triangles are
    1. The measure of the side opposite the 30° angle is one half the measure of the hypotenuse.
    2. The measure of the side opposite the 60° angle is one half the product of the measure of the hypotenuse and $\sqrt{3}$.

EXAMPLE:

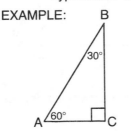

Since ABC is a 30-60-90 triangle, then $AC = \frac{1}{2}(AB)$ and $BC = \frac{1}{2}(AB\sqrt{3})$.

- **45-45-90 Triangles**
  The special properties of these isosceles right triangles are
    1. The measure of the hypotenuse is equal to the product of the measure of one of the equal legs and $\sqrt{2}$.
    2. The measure of either of the congruent legs is equal to the product of one half the measure of the hypotenuse and $\sqrt{2}$.

EXAMPLE:

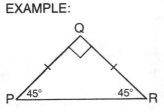

Since PQR is a 45-45-90 triangle with $\overline{PQ} \cong \overline{QR}$, then $PR = (PQ)\sqrt{2}$ and $PQ = \frac{1}{2}(PR)\sqrt{2}$.

CIRCLES

A *circle* is a set of points in a plane at a fixed distance from a fixed point in the plane.

5.1 Parts of Circles

The fixed point O in the plane is called the *center* of the circle. A circle is named by its center. If A is a point of the circle, then $\overline{OA}$ is called a *radius*. All radii (plural of "radius") in the same circle are congruent. A *diameter* is a line segment that passes through the center of the circle with its endpoints on the circle.

EXAMPLE:

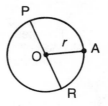

Name: Circle O
Radius: $\overline{OA}$
Diameter: $\overline{PR}$

5.2　Chord, Secant, and Tangent

- **Chord**
  A *chord* is a line segment whose endpoints are two distinct points of the circle.

- **Secant**
  A *secant* is a line segment or a ray that contains two distinct points of a circle.

- **Tangent**
  A line is *tangent* to a circle if it intersects the circle in exactly one point.

  EXAMPLES:

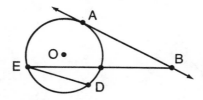

In circle O, $\overline{ED}$ is a chord, $\overline{BE}$ is a secant, and $\overleftrightarrow{AB}$ is a tangent.

5.3　Tangent Circles

Two circles are tangent to each other if they are both tangent to the same line at the same point.

EXAMPLES:

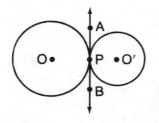

Externally tangent circles O and O′.

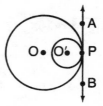

Internally tangent circles O and O′.

5.4 Tangents to a Circle

If a line is tangent to a circle, it is perpendicular to the radius drawn to the point of tangency.

EXAMPLE:

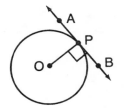

If $\overleftrightarrow{AB}$ is tangent to circle O at point P, then $\overleftrightarrow{AB} \perp \overline{OP}$.

Two tangents drawn to a circle from a point in the exterior of the circle are congruent and form congruent angles with a segment joining the point to the center of the circle.

EXAMPLE:

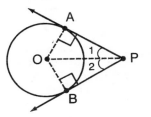

If $\overrightarrow{PA}$ and $\overrightarrow{PB}$ are tangent to circle O, then $\overline{PA} \cong \overline{PB}$ and $\angle 1 \cong \angle 2$.

5.5 Arcs of a Circle

An *arc* of a circle is any part of a circle and is named by its endpoints. The symbol ⌒ is used over the letters to identify the arc. An arc can be measured in degrees. The degree measure of a circle is 360.

EXAMPLE:

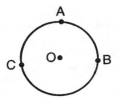

In circle O, $\overarc{AB}$ is less than a semicircle and is a *minor arc*. $\overarc{ACB}$ is greater than a semicircle and is a *major arc*.

- In each of the following figures, the numbered angle *intercepts* the arc highlighted.

43

EXAMPLES:

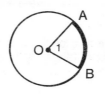 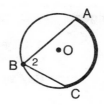

∠ AOB intercepts $\overarc{AB}$.　　∠ ABC intercepts $\overarc{AC}$.

- Parallel lines intercept equal arcs on a circle.

  EXAMPLE:

  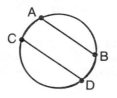

  If $\overline{AB} \parallel \overline{CD}$, then $m\overarc{AC} = m\overarc{BD}$.

5.6　Central Angle

A *central* angle of a circle is an angle whose vertex is the center of the circle. The degree measure of a minor arc of a circle is equal to the degree measure of its central angle.

EXAMPLE:

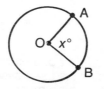

The measure of central angle AOB is x°, so $m\overarc{AB} = x°$.

5.7　Inscribed Angle

An *inscribed* angle is an angle determined by two chords of the circle which intersect on the circle. The measure of an inscribed angle is half the degree measure of its intercepted arc.

EXAMPLE:

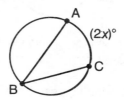

If $m\overarc{AC} = (2x)°$, then inscribed angle ABC = $\frac{1}{2}m\overarc{AC} = x°$.

- An angle inscribed in a semicircle is a right angle.

EXAMPLE:

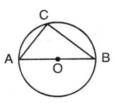

If ∠ C is inscribed in semicircle $\widehat{ACB}$, then m∠ C = 90°.

- If a quadrilateral is inscribed in a circle, the opposite angles are supplementary.

EXAMPLE:

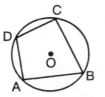

If quadrilateral ABCD is inscribed in circle O, then m∠ A + m∠ C = 180° and m∠ B + m∠ D = 180°.

5.8 Tangent, Chord, and Secant Angles

The measure of an angle formed by a tangent and a chord intersecting at the point of tangency is half the degree measure of the intercepted arc.

EXAMPLE:

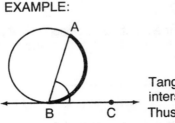

Tangent $\overleftrightarrow{BC}$ and chord $\overline{AB}$ intersect at B.
Thus, m∠ ABC = $\frac{1}{2}$m$\widehat{AB}$.

- **Two Chords**
The measure of an angle formed by two chords intersecting inside a circle is half the sum of the measures of its intercepted arcs.

EXAMPLE:

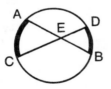

Chords $\overline{AB}$ and $\overline{CD}$ intersect at E.
Thus, m∠ DEB = $\frac{1}{2}$(m$\widehat{AC}$ + m$\widehat{DB}$)
and m∠ AEC = $\frac{1}{2}$(m$\widehat{AC}$ + m$\widehat{DB}$).

- **Two Tangents, Two Secants, Tangent and Secant**

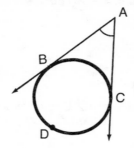

Tangents $\overrightarrow{AB}$ and $\overrightarrow{AC}$
$m\angle A = \frac{1}{2}(m\widehat{BDC} - m\widehat{BC})$

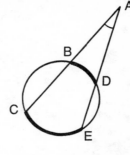

Secants $\overline{AC}$ and $\overline{AE}$
$m\angle A = \frac{1}{2}(m\widehat{CE} - m\widehat{BD})$

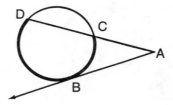

Tangent $\overrightarrow{AB}$ and Secant $\overline{AD}$
$m\angle A = \frac{1}{2}(m\widehat{BD} - m\widehat{BC})$

PERIMETER

Perimeter is the length of a closed curve such as the perimeter of a circle or the sum of the lengths of the sides of a polygon.

6.1 Polygons

The perimeter of a polygon is the sum of the measures of the sides of the polygon.

EXAMPLES:

Rhombus
$P = 4a$

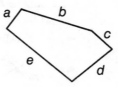

Pentagon
$P = a + b + c + d + e$

6.2 Triangles

The perimeter of a triangle is the sum of the measures of its sides.

EXAMPLES:

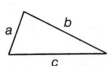

Scalene Triangle	Isosceles Triangle	Equilateral Triangle
$P = a + b + c$	$P = 2a + b$	$P = 3a$

6.3 Rectangles and Squares

These formulas can be used to find the perimeters of rectangles and squares.

EXAMPLES:

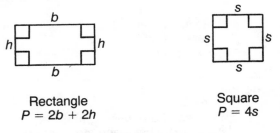

Rectangle
$P = 2b + 2h$

Square
$P = 4s$

6.4 Circle

The *circumference* of a circle is the length of the circle and is the product of pi (π) and the length of the diameter. Since the length of the diameter is twice the length of the radius, the circumference is the product of π and twice the length of the radius.

EXAMPLE:

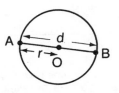

In circle O, diameter AB = d and radius AO = r,
so $C = \pi d$ or $C = 2\pi r$

AREA

The *area* of a closed polygonal region is determined by counting the number of unit regions that would fill the region. The unit of measure for area is the square unit (square inch, square meter, etc.). There are formulas for finding the area of special figures.

7.1 Rectangles and Squares

The area of a rectangle is equal to the product of the length of the base and the height drawn to that base.

The area of a square is equal to the square of the length of one of its sides.

EXAMPLES:

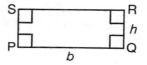

Rectangle PQRS has a base b and height h, so $A = bh$.

Square WXYZ has a side s, so $A = s^2$.

7.2 Parallelogram

The area of a parallelogram is equal to the product of the length of the base and the height drawn to that base.

EXAMPLE:

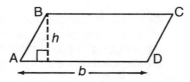

Parallelogram ABCD has a base b and height h, so $A = bh$.

7.3 Rhombus

The area of a rhombus can be found in the same way as the area of a parallelogram. In addition, the area of a rhombus is equal to one half the product of the lengths of its diagonals.

EXAMPLES:

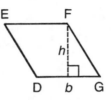

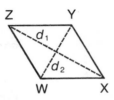

Rhombus DEFG has a base b and height h, so $A = bh$.

Rhombus WXYZ has diagonals d_1 and d_2, so $A = \frac{1}{2}d_1d_2$.

7.4 Trapezoid

The area of a trapezoid is equal to half the product of the length of its altitude and the sum of the lengths of its bases.

EXAMPLE:

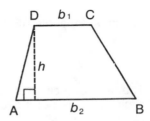

Trapezoid ABCD has bases b_1 and b_2 and an altitude h, so $A = \frac{1}{2}h(b_1 + b_2)$.

7.5 Triangles

The area of a triangle is equal to one half the product of the length of the base and the altitude to that base.

EXAMPLE:

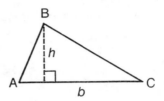

Triangle ABC has a base b and an altitude h, so $A = \frac{1}{2}bh$.

- **Right Triangle**
  The area of a right triangle is equal to one half the product of the lengths of its legs.

EXAMPLE:

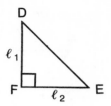

Right triangle DEF has legs ℓ_1 and ℓ_2, so $A = \frac{1}{2}\,\ell_1\ell_2$.

- **Equilateral Triangle**
  The area of an equilateral triangle is equal to one fourth the product of the square of the length of one of its sides and $\sqrt{3}$.

  EXAMPLE:

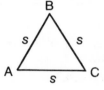

  Equilateral triangle ABC has sides of length s, so $A = \frac{s^2}{4}\sqrt{3}$.

7.6 Circle

The area of a circle is the measure of the region inside the circle. The area of a circle is the product of π and the square of the length of the radius.

EXAMPLE:

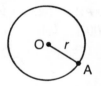

In circle O, radius $OA = r$, so $A = \pi r^2$.

- **Sector of a Circle**
  A *sector* of a circle is the region formed by two radii and its intercepted arc. The area of a sector is to the area of the circle as the angle of the sector is to 360°.

  EXAMPLE:

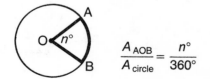

$$\frac{A_{AOB}}{A_{circle}} = \frac{n°}{360°}$$

- **Segment of a Circle**
  A *segment* of a circle is the region formed by a chord and its arc. The area of a segment may be found by subtracting the area of the triangle from the area of the sector.

EXAMPLE:

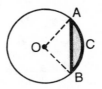

| Area of
segment ACB | = | Area of
sector OACB | − | Area of
triangle OAB |

7.7 Regular Polygon

Recall that a regular polygon is both equiangular and equilateral.

A circle can be *circumscribed* about any regular polygon (*n*-gon) and a circle can be *inscribed* in any regular polygon.

EXAMPLE:

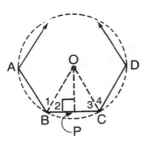

The center O of regular *n*-gon ABCD . . . is the common center of its inscribed and circumscribed circles.

The radius of a regular polygon is the distance from the center of the polygon to a vertex: radii $\overline{OA}$, $\overline{OB}$, $\overline{OC}$, $\overline{OD}$, . . .

The radius bisects the angle to which it is drawn. Thus, $\angle 1 \cong \angle 2 \cong \angle 3 \cong \angle 4 \ldots$

The *apothem* of a regular polygon is the perpendicular distance from the center of the polygon to a side. $\overline{OP}$ is an apothem.

A central angle ($\angle$ BOC) of an *n*-gon has a degree measure of $\frac{360}{n}$.

The *area* of a regular polygon is one half the product of the apothem and the perimeter.

EXAMPLE:

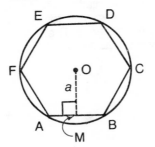

Regular hexagon ABCDEF has an apothem OM = *a* and a perimeter *p*, so $A = \frac{1}{2}ap$.

A *polyhedron* is a closed geometric surface formed by polygonal regions or *faces*. The intersection of the faces are called the *edges*. A *prism* is a polyhedron with two congruent and parallel faces called the *bases*. A *right prism* is a prism whose *lateral edges* are perpendicular to the bases.

EXAMPLES:

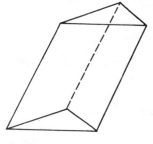 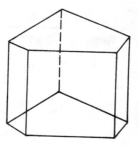

Oblique Prism   Right Prism

The *lateral area* of a prism is the sum of the areas of the lateral faces. The total surface area of the prism is the sum of its lateral areas and the areas of its bases.

EXAMPLE:

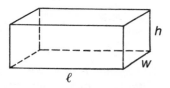

The area of the lateral faces is $2\ell h + 2hw$ and the area of its bases is $2\ell w$.

Thus, the total surface area S is $S = 2\ell h + 2hw + 2\ell w$, or $S = 2(\ell h + hw + \ell w)$.

VOLUME

Volume is the number of distinct unit volumes that would fill the region. The unit of measure for volume is the cubic unit (cubic inch, cubic meter, etc.). There are formulas for finding the volume of special figures.

8.1   Rectangular Prisms and Cubes

The volume V of a rectangular prism is equal to the product of the area of its base B and its height h.

The volume V of a cube is equal to the cube of its edge e.

EXAMPLES:

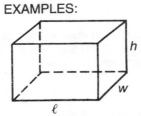

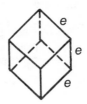

The rectangular prism has edges ℓ, w, and h, so $V = Bh$ or $V = \ell wh$.

The cube has an edge e, so $V = e^3$.

8.2   Other Solids

There are also formulas for finding the volume of a sphere, a right circular cylinder, a right circular cone, and a right triangular prism.

EXAMPLES:

Sphere
$V = \frac{4}{3}\pi r^3$

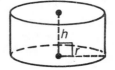

Right Circular Cylinder
$V = \pi r^2 h$

Right Circular Cone
$V = \frac{1}{3}\pi r^2 h$

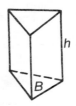

Right Triangular Prism
$B =$ area of the base, so
$V = Bh$

53

COORDINATE GEOMETRY

Coordinate or *Cartesian* geometry is a joining of two branches of mathematics, algebra and geometry.

9.1 Number Line

Each positive and negative number can be represented by a point on a straight line. Each point on the line can also be represented by a number.

EXAMPLES:

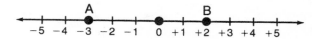

−3 is represented by point A.
Point B represents +2.

9.2 Set of Integers

Positive whole numbers, negative whole numbers, and zero make up the *set of integers*.

In the previous diagram, all points to the right of 0 represent positive integers and all those to the left of 0 represent negative integers.

The closed dot at 0 on the number line represents graphically the equality $x = 0$. The closed dots at −3 and +2 represent graphically the equalities, $x = -3$ and $x = +2$.

9.3 Inequalities

Inequalities with one variable can be shown on a number line. The graph of an inequality in one variable is the set of all points corresponding to the numbers belonging to the *solution set* of the inequality. An open dot indicates that the number corresponding to the point is *not* included in the solution set.

EXAMPLES:

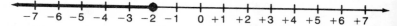

The graph above shows the solution set of $x \leq -2$.

The graph above shows the solution set of $x > 1$.

The graph above shows the solution set of the compound inequality $-3 \leq x \leq 3$.

9.4 Coordinate Plane

Points can be represented as pairs of numbers in a plane. Two number lines, at right angles to each other, are used to represent points in a plane. One number line is horizontal and is called the *x-axis*, the other is vertical and is called the *y-axis*. The two axes (plural of "axis") meet at the 0 point for each number line. This point is called the *origin*.

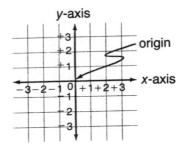

9.5 Ordered Pairs

A point in the plane can be named or located by a pair of numbers. The pair of numbers is called an *ordered pair*. To name a point by an ordered pair, first draw a perpendicular from the point to the *x*-axis. The number on the *x*-axis is called the *x-coordinate* of the point. Then draw a perpendicular from the point to the *y*-axis. The number on the *y*-axis is called the *y-coordinate* of the point.

To name the point, the *x*-coordinate is written first, and then the *y*-coordinate after it, in the form (x, y). The general form for labeling a point using a *coordinate pair* is P (x, y).

EXAMPLE: Locate points P, Q, R, and S with ordered pairs.

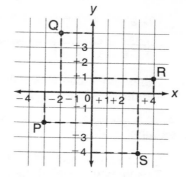

The figure above shows the location of points
P(−3, −2); Q(−2, +4); R(+4, +1); and S (+3, −4).

EXAMPLE: Graph the points whose ordered pairs are
(+2, +3) and (+3, +2).

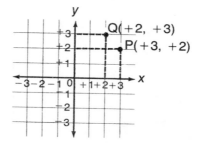

(+2, +3) locates point Q and (+3, +2) locates point P.

9.6   Points on the Axes

- (0, 0) is the ordered pair for the origin.
- The x-coordinate is 0 for any point on the y-axis.
- The y-coordinate is 0 for any point on the x-axis.

EXAMPLE:

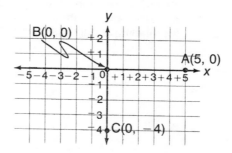

Point B, the origin, has coordinates (0, 0).
Point C, a point on the y-axis, has coordinates (0, −4).
Point A, a point on the x-axis, has coordinates (5, 0).

9.7 Distance Between Two Points

- **Using the Pythagorean Theorem**
  To measure the distance between two points in the
  coordinate plane, locate the ordered pair for each point, then
  draw vertical and horizontal lines to form a right triangle as
  shown below. Finally, use the Pythagorean theorem.

  EXAMPLE: Find the distance between A(−2, 4) and
  B(4, −4).

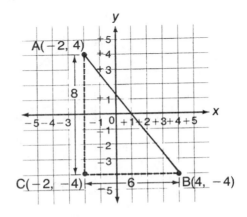

In right triangle ABC, $(AB)^2 = (AC)^2 + (CB)^2$
$(AB)^2 = 8^2 + 6^2$
$(AB)^2 = 64 + 36$
$(AB)^2 = 100$
$AB = 10$

- **Using the Distance Formula**
  The *distance formula* is a generalization of the Pythagorean
  theorem that can be used to find the distance d between
  any two points (x_1, y_1) and (x_2, y_2).
  $$d = \sqrt{(x_2 - x_1)^2 + (y_2 - y_1)^2}$$

  EXAMPLE: Find the distance between points (−2, 4)
  and (4, −4).
  Let (x_1, y_1) be (−2, 4) and (x_2, y_2) be (4, −4)

  Then, $\quad d = \sqrt{(x_2 - x_1)^2 + (y_2 - y_1)^2}$
  $d = \sqrt{[4 - (-2)]^2 + (-4 - 4)^2}$
  $d = \sqrt{(4 + 2)^2 + (-8)^2}$
  $d = \sqrt{6^2 + (-8)^2}$
  $d = \sqrt{36 + 64}$
  $d = \sqrt{100} = 10$

57

This answer agrees with the previous solution in which the Pythagorean theorem was used.

9.8 Equations of Circles

Some graphs can be expressed algebraically in the form of an equation with two variables.

A circle with its center at the origin and radius r has the equation $x^2 + y^2 = r^2$.

EXAMPLE: Write the equation of the circle that passes through (3, 4) and whose center is at the origin.

Use the distance formula to find the length of the radius.

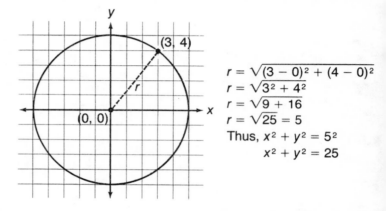

$$r = \sqrt{(3 - 0)^2 + (4 - 0)^2}$$
$$r = \sqrt{3^2 + 4^2}$$
$$r = \sqrt{9 + 16}$$
$$r = \sqrt{25} = 5$$
$$\text{Thus, } x^2 + y^2 = 5^2$$
$$x^2 + y^2 = 25$$

The circle with center (h, k) and radius r has the equation $(x - h)^2 + (y - k)^2 = r^2$.

EXAMPLE: What is the length of the radius and the coordinates of the center of the circle whose equation is $(x - 3)^2 + (y + 4)^2 = 36$?

Write the equation in the following form:
$$(x - h)^2 + (y - k)^2 = r^2$$
Thus, $\qquad (x - 3)^2 + [y - (-4)]^2 = 6^2$
Therefore, $h = 3$, $k = -4$ and $r = 6$.
The center is $(3, -4)$ and the length of the radius is 6.

EXAMPLE: Find the center and the radius of the circle whose equation is $x^2 - 4x + y^2 + 8y - 5 = 0$.

$$x^2 - 4x + y^2 + 8y - 5 = 0$$
Add 5 to both sides.
$$x^2 - 4x + y^2 + 8y = 5$$
Complete the square.
$$x^2 - 4x + 4 + y^2 + 8y + 16 = 5 + 4 + 16$$
Factor.
$$(x - 2)^2 + (y + 4)^2 = 25$$

Thus, $h = 2$, $k = -4$, and $r = 5$.
The center is $(2, -4)$ and the length of the radius is 5.

9.9 Midpoint Formulas

The midpoint of the segment joining the points (x_1, y_1) and (x_2, y_2) is the point $(\bar{x}, \bar{y})$ where $\bar{x} = \frac{x_1 + x_2}{2}$ and $\bar{y} = \frac{y_1 + y_2}{2}$.

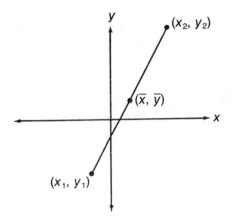

EXAMPLE: In $\triangle ABC$, median $\overline{BD}$ meets side $\overline{AC}$ at point D. If the coordinates of point A are (7, 6) and of point C are (9, −2), find the coordinates of point D.

Since the median of a triangle is a line segment joining a vertex to the midpoint of the opposite side, D is the midpoint of $\overline{AC}$.

Let (7, 6) be (x_1, y_1) and (9, −2) be (x_2, y_2).

Thus, $\bar{x} = \frac{7 + 9}{2} = 8$ and $\bar{y} = \frac{6 - 2}{2} = 2$. The coordinates of D are (8, 2).

EXAMPLE: The coordinates of the center of circle O are (−7, 6). The coordinates of diameter $\overline{AB}$ are A(2, −4) and B(−16, y). What is the value of y?

Use the formulas $\bar{x} = \frac{x_1 + x_2}{2}$ and $\bar{y} = \frac{y_1 + y_2}{2}$.

We need only the formula for $\bar{y}$, so
$$6 = \frac{-4 + y}{2}$$

Multiply both sides by 2.
$$2(6) = \overset{1}{\cancel{2}} \left[\frac{(-4 + y)}{\underset{1}{\cancel{2}}} \right]$$

$$12 = -4 + y$$

Add 4 to both sides.
$$16 = y$$

59

9.10 Slope of a Line

The *slope* of a line segment is the ratio of the difference of the y-coordinates to the difference of the corresponding x-coordinates.

The slope m of a line segment whose endpoints are points (x_1, y_1) and (x_2, y_2) where $x_2 \neq x_1$, is

$$m = \frac{y_2 - y_1}{x_2 - x_1}$$

EXAMPLE: What is the slope of a line that passes through the points A($-$2, 3) and B(5, $-$4)?

Let A($-$2, 3) be (x_1, y_1) and B(5, $-$4) be (x_2, y_2).

Use the following formula:

$$m = \frac{y_2 - y_1}{x_2 - x_1}$$

$$m = \frac{-4 - 3}{5 - (-2)}$$

$$= \frac{-7}{7} = -1$$

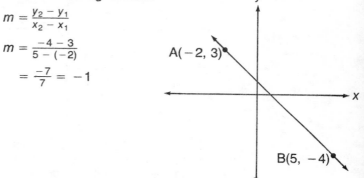

If the slope of a line is *negative*, the line slants downward from left to right.

EXAMPLE: What is the slope of a line that passes through the points M($-$3,$-$4) and N(1, 1)?

Let M($-$3,$-$4) be (x_1, y_1) and N(1, 1) be (x_2, y_2).

Use the following formula:

$$m = \frac{y_2 - y_1}{x_2 - x_1}$$

$$m = \frac{1 - (-4)}{1 - (-3)} = \frac{5}{4}$$

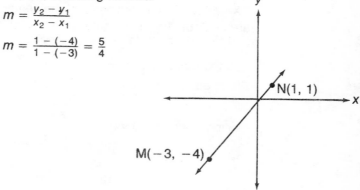

A line with a *positive* slope slants upward from left to right. If $y_2 = y_1$, then the slope is 0. The slope of a horizontal line is 0.

If $x_2 = x_1$, and division by 0 is undefined, the slope is not defined for a vertical line.

9.11 Parallel and Perpendicular Lines

- **Parallel Lines**

  Two lines are parallel if and only if they have equal slopes, $m_1 = m_2$. The phrase *if and only if* includes the statement and its converse.

  EXAMPLE: The coordinates of the vertices of quadrilateral ABCD are A(-1, 0), B(1, 1), C(0, 3) and D(-3, 4). Show that $\overline{BC} \parallel \overline{AD}$.

  Find the slopes of $\overline{BC}$ and $\overline{AD}$. If the slopes are equal, the line segments are parallel.

  Let B(1, 1) be (x_1, y_1) and C(0, 3) be (x_2, y_2).

  $$m = \frac{y_2 - y_1}{x_2 - x_1}$$

  $$m_1 = \frac{3 - 1}{0 - 1} = \frac{2}{-1} = -2$$

  Let D(-3, 4) be (x_1, y_1) and A(-1, 0) be (x_2, y_2).

  $$m_2 = \frac{0 - 4}{-1 - (-3)} = \frac{-4}{2} = -2$$

  Thus, $m_1 = m_2$ and $\overline{BC} \parallel \overline{AD}$.

- **Perpendicular Lines**

  Two lines are perpendicular if and only if the slope of one line is the negative reciprocal of the slope of the other line.

  $$m_1 = \frac{-1}{m_2} \text{ or } m_1 \cdot m_2 = -1$$

  EXAMPLE: The coordinates of the vertices of $\triangle ABC$ are A(-1, 2), B(x, 8), and C(5, -2). Find the value of x so that $\angle BAC$ is a right angle.

  For $\angle BAC$ to be a right angle, $\overline{AB}$ must be perpendicular to $\overline{AC}$. The slope of $\overline{AB}$, m_1, must be the negative reciprocal of the slope of $\overline{AC}$, m_2.

  Find the slope of $\overline{AB}$ in terms of x.
  Let A(-1, 2) be (x_1, y_1) and B(x, 8) be (x_2, y_2).

  $$m = \frac{y_2 - y_1}{x_2 - x_1}$$

  $$m_1 = \frac{8 - 2}{x - (-1)} = \frac{6}{x + 1}$$

Find the slope of $\overline{AC}$.
Let $A(-1, 2)$ be (x_1, y_1) and $C(5, -2)$ be (x_2, y_2).

$$m_2 = \frac{-2 - 2}{5 - (-1)} = \frac{-4}{6} \text{ or } \frac{-2}{3}$$

If the lines are perpendicular, solve for x using $m_1 \cdot m_2 = -1$.

$$\frac{\overset{2}{\cancel{6}}}{x + 1} \cdot \frac{-2}{\underset{1}{\cancel{3}}} = -1$$

$$\frac{-4}{x + 1} = -1$$

$$-4 = -x - 1$$

$$x = 3$$

9.12 Equations of Lines

The graph of any equation that can be written in the form $ax + by + c = 0$, where a and b are not both 0, is a line.

● **Slope-Intercept Form**

The y-intercept is the y-coordinate of the point where the line crosses the y-axis.

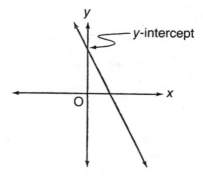

The equation of a line with slope m and y-intercept b is $y = mx + b$.

EXAMPLE: Write the equation of the line containing points (3, 2) and (6, 8).

First, find the slope of the line.
Let (3, 2) be (x_1, y_1) and (6, 8) be (x_2, y_2).

$$m = \frac{y_2 - y_1}{x_2 - x_1}$$

$$m = \frac{8 - 2}{6 - 3} = \frac{6}{3} = 2$$

Then, write the equation of the line.

Thus, $y = mx + b$ becomes $y = 2x + b$.

Since the coordinates of a point on the line satisfy the equation of the line, substitute either (3, 2) or (6, 8) for x and y in $y = 2x + b$ and solve for b.

For (3, 2)
$$2 = 2(3) + b$$
$$2 = 6 + b$$
$$-4 = b$$

Thus, the equation of the line is $y = 2x - 4$.

- **Point-Slope Form**
  The equation of a line passing through a point (x_1, y_1) and having slope m is $y - y_1 = m(x - x_1)$.

EXAMPLE: Write the equation of the line that passes through the point (0, 4) and is parallel to the line $y = -\frac{1}{2}x + 3$.

If the line is parallel to $y = -\frac{1}{2}x + 3$, the slopes of both lines are equal. Therefore, $m = -\frac{1}{2}$. Since it is known that the line passes through point (0, 4), use the point-slope form to find the equation.

$$y - y_1 = m(x - x_1)$$
$$y - 4 = -\frac{1}{2}(x - 0)$$
$$y - 4 = -\frac{1}{2}x$$
$$2(y - 4) = 2(-\frac{1}{2}x)$$
$$2y - 8 = -x$$
$$x + 2y = 8$$

EXAMPLE: Write the equation of the line that passes through the point $(-1, -2)$ and is perpendicular to the line $y = -3x + 5$.

The slope of the line $y = -3x + 5$ is -3. If a line is perpendicular to $y = -3x + 5$, the slope of one is the negative reciprocal of the other. Therefore, the slope of the desired line is $\frac{1}{3}$ since $(-3)\left(\frac{1}{3}\right) = -1$.

Use the point-slope form to find the equation.

$$y - y_1 = m(x - x_1)$$
$$y - (-2) = \frac{1}{3}[x - (-1)]$$
$$y + 2 = \frac{1}{3}(x + 1)$$
$$3(y + 2) = x + 1$$
$$3y + 6 = x + 1$$
$$x - 3y = 5$$

PROBLEM SOLVING

Although there is no general method for attacking geometry problems, these are some suggestions that should help you in solving problems.

- Draw a diagram to illustrate the problem.
- Examine the diagram for clues.
- Draw additional line segments to the given diagram to obtain more information.
- Try breaking the problem up into smaller parts.
- Divide the figure up into parts.
- Use a formula, if applicable, to find perimeter, area, or volume.

10.1   Angles

If three lines intersect, as in the figure at the right, to form the angles shown, then find $a + b$ in terms of y.

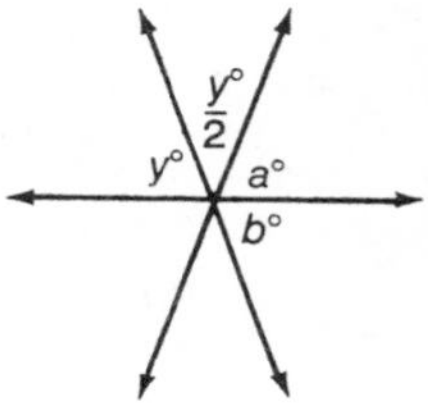

Since the sum of the degree measures of angles formed by opposite rays is 180, then

$$\frac{y}{2} + a + b = 180$$
$$a + b = 180 - \frac{y}{2}$$

10.2   Lines

In the figure at the right, two parallel lines $\overrightarrow{AB}$ and $\overrightarrow{CD}$ are cut by transversal $\overrightarrow{EF}$ intersecting $\overrightarrow{AB}$ in G and $\overrightarrow{CD}$ in H.

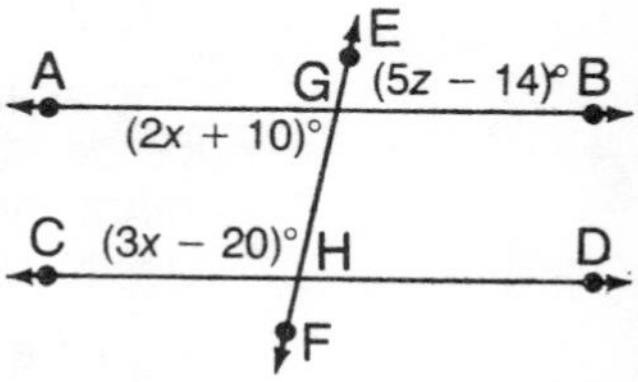

If m $\angle$ AGH = $(2x + 10)°$, m $\angle$ CHG = $(3x - 20)°$, and m $\angle$ EGB = $(5z - 14)°$, find the value of z.

If a transversal cuts two parallel lines, the consecutive interior angles are supplementary.

$$\text{m} \angle \text{AGH} + \text{m} \angle \text{CHG} = 180°$$
$$(2x + 10)° + (3x - 20)° = 180°$$
$$5x - 10 = 180$$
$$5x = 190$$
$$x = 38$$

$$\text{m} \angle \text{AGH} = (2x + 10)° = [2(38) + (10)]° = 86°$$

Since the measures of two vertical angles are equal,

$$m \angle AGH = m \angle EGB$$
$$86° = (5z - 14)°$$
$$86 = 5z - 14$$
$$100 = 5z$$
$$20 = z$$

10.3 Polygons

If x is the measure of one angle of a regular hexagon and y is the measure of one angle of a regular octagon, then find the ratio of x to y.

In a regular polygon of n sides, the measure of one angle is $\frac{(n - 2)180°}{n}$.

In a regular hexagon, $n = 6$: $\frac{(6 - 2)180°}{6} = \frac{4(180)°}{6} = 120°$.

In a regular octagon, $n = 8$: $\frac{(8 - 2)180°}{8} = \frac{6(180)°}{8} = 135°$.

Thus, $\frac{x}{y} = \frac{120°}{135°} = \frac{8}{9}$.

10.4 Triangles

If a person were to cut five circles, each 2 cm in diameter, from a rectangular piece of cardboard 6 cm long, at least how many centimeters wide would the piece of cardboard have to be?

Draw a diagram to illustrate the problem.

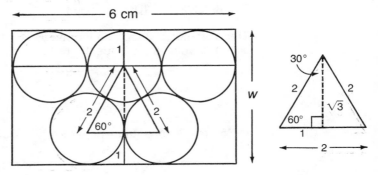

The five circles will fit into the rectangle as shown above. The enlarged triangle at the right is divided into two 30-60-90 triangles. This yields an altitude equal to $\sqrt{3}$. The width w of the rectangle is $1 + \sqrt{3} + 1 = 2 + \sqrt{3}$.

10.5　Circles

Chord AC is tangent to circle E at point B. If the radius of circle D is 15 and AC = 18, what is the radius of circle E?

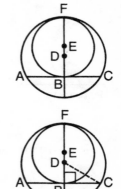

Draw the line segment DC. Let r represent the radius of circle E. Since $\overline{AC}$ is tangent to circle E at point B, DBC is a right angle and $\overline{FB}$ is the perpendicular bisector of $\overline{AC}$. Therefore, BC = 9.

Use the Pythagorean theorem to find BD. If BC = 9 and DC = 15, then BD = 12.

$$BF = 2r = BD + DF$$
$$2r = 12 + 15$$
$$2r = 27$$
$$r = 13\tfrac{1}{2}$$

The radius of circle E is $13\tfrac{1}{2}$.

10.6　Perimeter

How far would an automobile wheel of diameter 2 feet roll in 350 revolutions? (Use $\pi \approx \frac{22}{7}$.)

The diameter is 2 feet, so the radius is 1 foot. The circumference is 2π times the radius.

$$C = 2\pi r$$
$$C = 2 \times \tfrac{22}{7} \times 1$$
$$C = \tfrac{44}{7} \text{ feet}$$

In 350 revolutions, the wheel rolls $\frac{44}{7} \times 350$ or 2200 feet.

10.7　Area

What is the area of the rectangle needed to completely enclose four circles each with an area of $\frac{\pi a^2}{4}$?

Since $A = \pi r^2$ and the area of each circle is $\frac{\pi a^2}{4}$, then the radius of each circle is $\frac{a}{2}$. If a circle has a radius of $\frac{a}{2}$, it needs a square of area a^2 to completely enclose it.

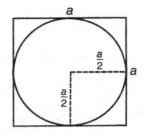

Four such circles need four such rectangles to completely enclose them, forming a square of area $4a^2$.

10.8 Volume

In the figure shown at the right, if the outer cylinder has radius R and the inner cylinder has radius r, what is the volume of the shaded region?

The volume V of a right circular cylinder of radius r and height h is given by the formula $V = \pi r^2 h$.

The volume of the outer cylinder of radius R is $V = \pi R^2 h$.

The volume of the inner cylinder of radius r is $V = \pi r^2 h$.

Therefore,

Volume of shaded = Volume of outer − Volume of inner
region   cylinder   cylinder

$$V = \pi R^2 h - \pi r^2 h$$
$$V = \pi h(R^2 - r^2)$$

10.9 Coordinate Geometry

Triangle ABC has vertices A(-1, 2), B(3, 8), and C(5, -2). Find the area of triangle ABC.

Enclose △ABC in a rectangle by drawing two horizontal lines and two vertical lines as shown in the figure. Then use the triangles and the rectangle formed to find the area of △ABC.

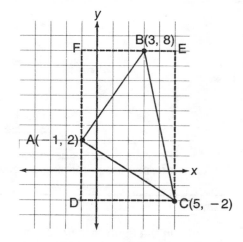

Area of △ABC = Area of rectangle DCEF − (Area of △ADC + Area of △BEC + Area of △BFA)

Area of rectangle DCEF = 6(10) or 60

The triangles are right triangles so use the formula $A = \frac{1}{2}\ell_1\ell_2$.

Area of △ADC = $\frac{1}{2}$(4)(6) = 12

Area of △BEC = $\frac{1}{2}$(2)(10) = 10

Area of △BFA = $\frac{1}{2}$(4)(6) = 12

Area of △ABC = 60 − (12 + 10 + 12)
= 60 − 34
= 26

10.10 Combining Strategies

In a circle with radius r, a rectangle is inscribed in one quadrant. What is the length of diagonal $\overline{AC}$?

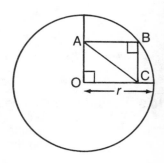

Draw the other diagonal $\overline{OB}$. $\overline{OB}$ is a radius of the circle with length r. Since the diagonals of a rectangle are congruent, $\overline{OB} \cong \overline{AC}$. Therefore AC must also equal the length of the radius r.

Part Three

Practice Tests in Specific Geometry Areas

This section has practice tests for each of the ten areas found in the Geometry Refresher Section.

Use the appropriate Answer Sheet on pages 70-73 to record your answers.

After you have completed each test, you can check your answers using the Answer Keys on pages 94-96. Each answer is referenced to the appropriate Geometry Refresher Section. The references, in parentheses, follow the answer and are in the same form as in the Answer Key to the Diagnostic Tests.

The solutions, with error anlaysis for each problem, begin on page 97.

Areas	Pages		
	Answer Sheet	Test	Answer Key
Angles	70	74	94
Lines	70	76	94
Polygons	70	78	95
Triangles	71	80	95
Circles	71	82	95
Perimeter	71	84	95
Area	72	86	96
Volume	72	88	96
Coordinate Geometry	73	90	96
Problem Solving	73	92	96

Answer Sheets
Practice Tests

ANGLES

1. Ⓐ Ⓑ Ⓒ Ⓓ
2. Ⓐ Ⓑ Ⓒ Ⓓ
3. Ⓐ Ⓑ Ⓒ Ⓓ
4. Ⓐ Ⓑ Ⓒ Ⓓ
5. Ⓐ Ⓑ Ⓒ Ⓓ
6. Ⓐ Ⓑ Ⓒ Ⓓ
7. Ⓐ Ⓑ Ⓒ Ⓓ
8. Ⓐ Ⓑ Ⓒ Ⓓ

9. Ⓐ Ⓑ Ⓒ Ⓓ
10. Ⓐ Ⓑ Ⓒ Ⓓ
11. Ⓐ Ⓑ Ⓒ Ⓓ
12. Ⓐ Ⓑ Ⓒ Ⓓ
13. Ⓐ Ⓑ Ⓒ Ⓓ
14. Ⓐ Ⓑ Ⓒ Ⓓ
15. Ⓐ Ⓑ Ⓒ Ⓓ

LINES

1. Ⓐ Ⓑ Ⓒ Ⓓ
2. Ⓐ Ⓑ Ⓒ Ⓓ
3. Ⓐ Ⓑ Ⓒ Ⓓ
4. Ⓐ Ⓑ Ⓒ Ⓓ
5. Ⓐ Ⓑ Ⓒ Ⓓ
6. Ⓐ Ⓑ Ⓒ Ⓓ
7. Ⓐ Ⓑ Ⓒ Ⓓ
8. Ⓐ Ⓑ Ⓒ Ⓓ

9. Ⓐ Ⓑ Ⓒ Ⓓ
10. Ⓐ Ⓑ Ⓒ Ⓓ
11. Ⓐ Ⓑ Ⓒ Ⓓ
12. Ⓐ Ⓑ Ⓒ Ⓓ
13. Ⓐ Ⓑ Ⓒ Ⓓ
14. Ⓐ Ⓑ Ⓒ Ⓓ
15. Ⓐ Ⓑ Ⓒ Ⓓ

POLYGONS

1. Ⓐ Ⓑ Ⓒ Ⓓ
2. Ⓐ Ⓑ Ⓒ Ⓓ
3. Ⓐ Ⓑ Ⓒ Ⓓ
4. Ⓐ Ⓑ Ⓒ Ⓓ
5. Ⓐ Ⓑ Ⓒ Ⓓ
6. Ⓐ Ⓑ Ⓒ Ⓓ
7. Ⓐ Ⓑ Ⓒ Ⓓ
8. Ⓐ Ⓑ Ⓒ Ⓓ

9. Ⓐ Ⓑ Ⓒ Ⓓ
10. Ⓐ Ⓑ Ⓒ Ⓓ
11. Ⓐ Ⓑ Ⓒ Ⓓ
12. Ⓐ Ⓑ Ⓒ Ⓓ
13. Ⓐ Ⓑ Ⓒ Ⓓ
14. Ⓐ Ⓑ Ⓒ Ⓓ
15. Ⓐ Ⓑ Ⓒ Ⓓ

TRIANGLES

1. (A) (B) (C) (D)
2. (A) (B) (C) (D)
3. (A) (B) (C) (D)
4. (A) (B) (C) (D)
5. (A) (B) (C) (D)
6. (A) (B) (C) (D)
7. (A) (B) (C) (D)
8. (A) (B) (C) (D)

9. (A) (B) (C) (D)
10. (A) (B) (C) (D)
11. (A) (B) (C) (D)
12. (A) (B) (C) (D)
13. (A) (B) (C) (D)
14. (A) (B) (C) (D)
15. (A) (B) (C) (D)

CIRCLES

1. (A) (B) (C) (D)
2. (A) (B) (C) (D)
3. (A) (B) (C) (D)
4. (A) (B) (C) (D)
5. (A) (B) (C) (D)
6. (A) (B) (C) (D)
7. (A) (B) (C) (D)
8. (A) (B) (C) (D)

9. (A) (B) (C) (D)
10. (A) (B) (C) (D)
11. (A) (B) (C) (D)
12. (A) (B) (C) (D)
13. (A) (B) (C) (D)
14. (A) (B) (C) (D)
15. (A) (B) (C) (D)

PERIMETER

1. (A) (B) (C) (D)
2. (A) (B) (C) (D)
3. (A) (B) (C) (D)
4. (A) (B) (C) (D)
5. (A) (B) (C) (D)
6. (A) (B) (C) (D)
7. (A) (B) (C) (D)
8. (A) (B) (C) (D)

9. (A) (B) (C) (D)
10. (A) (B) (C) (D)
11. (A) (B) (C) (D)
12. (A) (B) (C) (D)
13. (A) (B) (C) (D)
14. (A) (B) (C) (D)
15. (A) (B) (C) (D)

AREA

1. Ⓐ Ⓑ Ⓒ Ⓓ
2. Ⓐ Ⓑ Ⓒ Ⓓ
3. Ⓐ Ⓑ Ⓒ Ⓓ
4. Ⓐ Ⓑ Ⓒ Ⓓ
5. Ⓐ Ⓑ Ⓒ Ⓓ
6. Ⓐ Ⓑ Ⓒ Ⓓ
7. Ⓐ Ⓑ Ⓒ Ⓓ
8. Ⓐ Ⓑ Ⓒ Ⓓ

9. Ⓐ Ⓑ Ⓒ Ⓓ
10. Ⓐ Ⓑ Ⓒ Ⓓ
11. Ⓐ Ⓑ Ⓒ Ⓓ
12. Ⓐ Ⓑ Ⓒ Ⓓ
13. Ⓐ Ⓑ Ⓒ Ⓓ
14. Ⓐ Ⓑ Ⓒ Ⓓ
15. Ⓐ Ⓑ Ⓒ Ⓓ

VOLUME

1. Ⓐ Ⓑ Ⓒ Ⓓ
2. Ⓐ Ⓑ Ⓒ Ⓓ
3. Ⓐ Ⓑ Ⓒ Ⓓ
4. Ⓐ Ⓑ Ⓒ Ⓓ
5. Ⓐ Ⓑ Ⓒ Ⓓ
6. Ⓐ Ⓑ Ⓒ Ⓓ
7. Ⓐ Ⓑ Ⓒ Ⓓ
8. Ⓐ Ⓑ Ⓒ Ⓓ

9. Ⓐ Ⓑ Ⓒ Ⓓ
10. Ⓐ Ⓑ Ⓒ Ⓓ
11. Ⓐ Ⓑ Ⓒ Ⓓ
12. Ⓐ Ⓑ Ⓒ Ⓓ
13. Ⓐ Ⓑ Ⓒ Ⓓ
14. Ⓐ Ⓑ Ⓒ Ⓓ
15. Ⓐ Ⓑ Ⓒ Ⓓ

COORDINATE GEOMETRY

1. (A) (B) (C) (D)
2. (A) (B) (C) (D)
3. (A) (B) (C) (D)
4. (A) (B) (C) (D)
5. (A) (B) (C) (D)
6. (A) (B) (C) (D)
7. (A) (B) (C) (D)
8. (A) (B) (C) (D)

9. (A) (B) (C) (D)
10. (A) (B) (C) (D)
11. (A) (B) (C) (D)
12. (A) (B) (C) (D)
13. (A) (B) (C) (D)
14. (A) (B) (C) (D)
15. (A) (B) (C) (D)

PROBLEM SOLVING

1. (A) (B) (C) (D)
2. (A) (B) (C) (D)
3. (A) (B) (C) (D)
4. (A) (B) (C) (D)
5. (A) (B) (C) (D)
6. (A) (B) (C) (D)
7. (A) (B) (C) (D)
8. (A) (B) (C) (D)

9. (A) (B) (C) (D)
10. (A) (B) (C) (D)
11. (A) (B) (C) (D)
12. (A) (B) (C) (D)
13. (A) (B) (C) (D)
14. (A) (B) (C) (D)
15. (A) (B) (C) (D)

Geometry Practice Tests

ANGLES

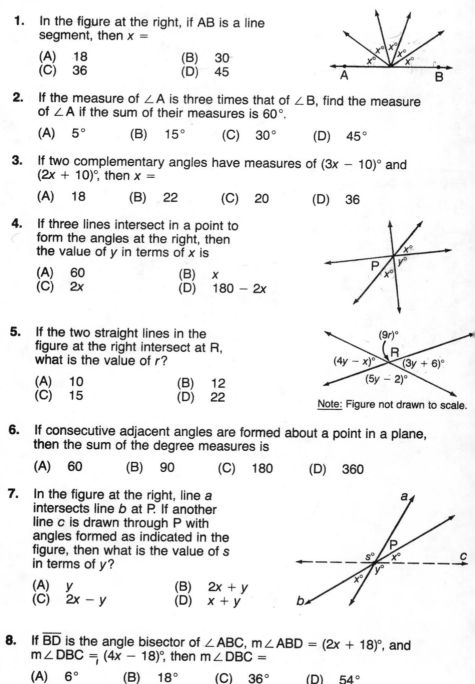

1. In the figure at the right, if AB is a line segment, then $x =$

    (A) 18 (B) 30
    (C) 36 (D) 45

2. If the measure of $\angle A$ is three times that of $\angle B$, find the measure of $\angle A$ if the sum of their measures is $60°$.

    (A) $5°$ (B) $15°$ (C) $30°$ (D) $45°$

3. If two complementary angles have measures of $(3x - 10)°$ and $(2x + 10)°$, then $x =$

    (A) 18 (B) 22 (C) 20 (D) 36

4. If three lines intersect in a point to form the angles at the right, then the value of y in terms of x is

    (A) 60 (B) x
    (C) $2x$ (D) $180 - 2x$

5. If the two straight lines in the figure at the right intersect at R, what is the value of r?

    (A) 10 (B) 12
    (C) 15 (D) 22

    Note: Figure not drawn to scale.

6. If consecutive adjacent angles are formed about a point in a plane, then the sum of the degree measures is

    (A) 60 (B) 90 (C) 180 (D) 360

7. In the figure at the right, line a intersects line b at P. If another line c is drawn through P with angles formed as indicated in the figure, then what is the value of s in terms of y?

    (A) y (B) $2x + y$
    (C) $2x - y$ (D) $x + y$

8. If $\overline{BD}$ is the angle bisector of $\angle ABC$, $m\angle ABD = (2x + 18)°$, and $m\angle DBC = (4x - 18)°$, then $m\angle DBC =$

    (A) $6°$ (B) $18°$ (C) $36°$ (D) $54°$

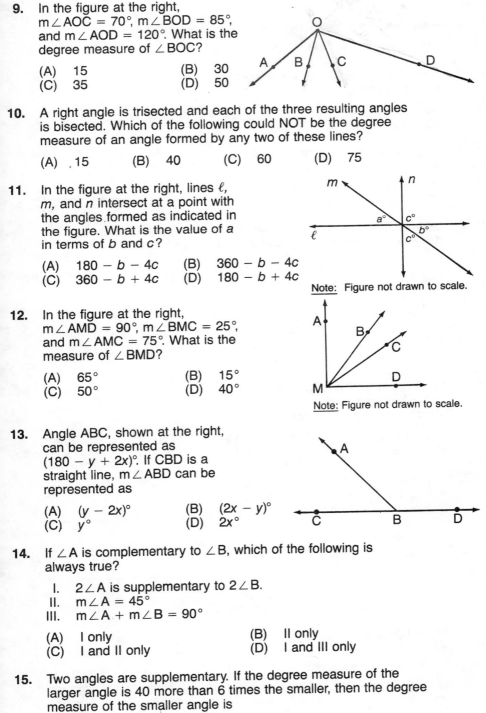

9. In the figure at the right,
$m \angle AOC = 70°$, $m \angle BOD = 85°$,
and $m \angle AOD = 120°$. What is the
degree measure of $\angle BOC$?

(A) 15   (B) 30
(C) 35   (D) 50

10. A right angle is trisected and each of the three resulting angles
is bisected. Which of the following could NOT be the degree
measure of an angle formed by any two of these lines?

(A) 15   (B) 40   (C) 60   (D) 75

11. In the figure at the right, lines ℓ,
m, and n intersect at a point with
the angles formed as indicated in
the figure. What is the value of a
in terms of b and c?

(A) $180 - b - 4c$ (B) $360 - b - 4c$
(C) $360 - b + 4c$ (D) $180 - b + 4c$

Note: Figure not drawn to scale.

12. In the figure at the right,
$m \angle AMD = 90°$, $m \angle BMC = 25°$,
and $m \angle AMC = 75°$. What is the
measure of $\angle BMD$?

(A) 65°   (B) 15°
(C) 50°   (D) 40°

Note: Figure not drawn to scale.

13. Angle ABC, shown at the right,
can be represented as
$(180 - y + 2x)°$. If CBD is a
straight line, $m \angle ABD$ can be
represented as

(A) $(y - 2x)°$ (B) $(2x - y)°$
(C) $y°$ (D) $2x°$

14. If $\angle A$ is complementary to $\angle B$, which of the following is
always true?

I. $2\angle A$ is supplementary to $2\angle B$.
II. $m \angle A = 45°$
III. $m \angle A + m \angle B = 90°$

(A) I only   (B) II only
(C) I and II only   (D) I and III only

15. Two angles are supplementary. If the degree measure of the
larger angle is 40 more than 6 times the smaller, then the degree
measure of the smaller angle is

(A) 20   (B) 28   (C) $31\frac{3}{7}$ (D) 160

LINES

1. If two lines are perpendicular, then they intersect in how many points?

   (A)   0   (B)   1   (C)   2   (D)   4

2. If two lines intersect and form congruent adjacent angles, then the lines are

   (A)   congruent   (B)   parallel
   (C)   perpendicular   (D)   vertical

3. In the figure at the right, $\overleftrightarrow{LM} \parallel \overleftrightarrow{NP}$, $m\angle 1 = 65°$, and $m\angle 2 = 50°$. Then $m\angle 3$ is

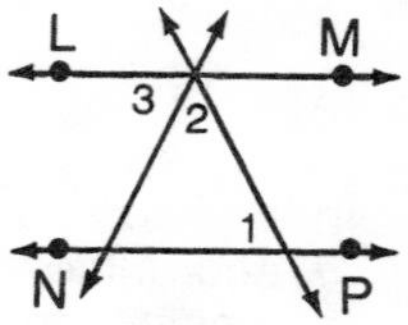

   (A)   50°   (B)   65°
   (C)   115°   (D)   130°

4. What is the least number of distinct lines in a plane that can be drawn so that the total number of points of intersection is 6?

   (A)   3   (B)   4   (C)   5   (D)   6

5. In the figure at the right, if $\ell \parallel m$, $a = 65$, and $c = 45$, then $b - c =$

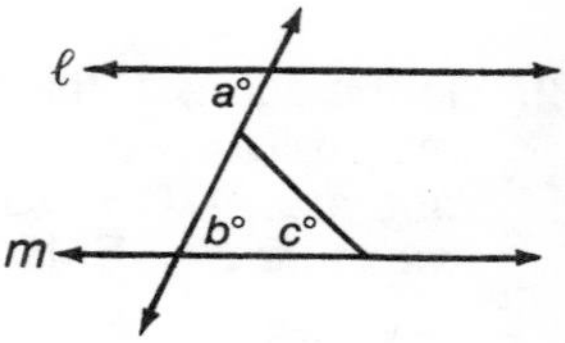

   (A)   0   (B)   20
   (C)   65   (D)   70

6. In the figure at the right, ℓ, m, and n are lines with $n \perp m$. Which angles are congruent?

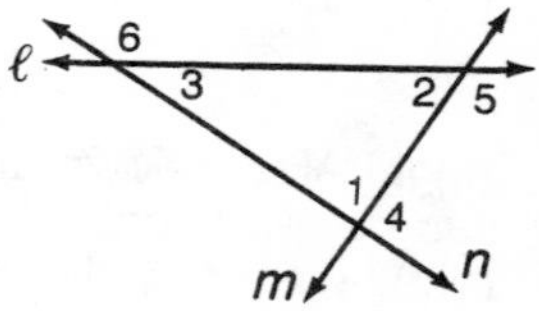

   (A)   1 and 3   (B)   2 and 6
   (C)   2 and 3   (D)   1 and 4

7. In the diagram at the right, if $\ell_1 \parallel \ell_2$, $\ell_2 \parallel \ell_3$, and $\ell_1 \perp \ell_4$, which of the following statements must be true?

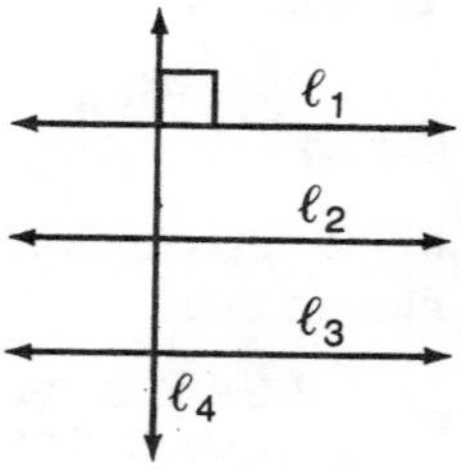

   I. $\ell_1 \parallel \ell_3$

   II. $\ell_2 \perp \ell_4$

   III. $\ell_3 \perp \ell_4$

   (A)   I only   (B)   II only
   (C)   I and II only   (D)   I, II, and III

8. In the figure at the right, B is the midpoint of $\overline{AC}$, D is the midpoint of $\overline{CE}$, and BD = 18. AE =

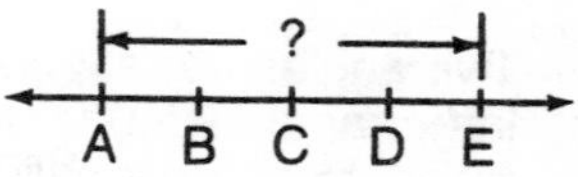

   (A)   27   (B)   36
   (C)   45   (D)   54

76

9. In the figure at the right, if $\overline{AB} \parallel \overline{CD}$ and $\overline{CB}$ is a line segment, then $x =$

(A) 75   (B) 80
(C) 85   (D) 105

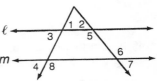

10. In the figure at the right, $\ell \parallel m$. Which of the following pairs of angles are NOT supplementary?

(A) 1 and 8   (B) 2 and 6
(C) 3 and 4   (D) 5 and 7

11. In the figure at the right, what is the greatest number of nonoverlapping regions into which the shaded region can be divided with exactly two lines?

(A) 2   (B) 3
(C) 4   (D) 5

12. In the figure at the right, ℓ_1 and ℓ_2 meet when extended to the right. What is the sum of x and y?

(A) less than 180
(B) equal to 180
(C) greater than 180
(D) It cannot be determined from the information given.

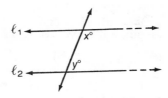

13. In the figure at the right, $\ell_1 \parallel \ell_2$ and $x = y = 90$. What is the relationship between $\overline{PQ}$ and $\overline{RS}$?

(A) PQ < RS
(B) PQ = RS
(C) PQ > RS
(D) It cannot be determined from the information given.

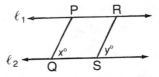

Note: Figure not drawn to scale.

14. In the figure at the right, $\overrightarrow{BA} \perp \overrightarrow{BC}$ and $\overrightarrow{BD}$ is drawn. If $m\angle ABD = (3x - 5)°$ and $m\angle CBD = (5x - 17)°$, then $m\angle ABD =$

(A) $14°$ (B) $20\frac{1}{2}°$
(C) $37°$ (D) $53°$

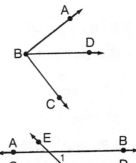

15. In the figure at the right, $\overleftrightarrow{AB} \parallel \overleftrightarrow{CD}$, $\overrightarrow{EF}$ is a transversal, $m\angle 1 = (2x + 10)°$, and $m\angle 2 = (3x - 20)°$. Find $m\angle 2$.

(A) $30°$ (B) $38°$
(C) $86°$ (D) $94°$

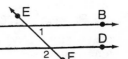

POLYGONS

1. In rhombus ABCD, if AB = 6x + 1 and BC = x + 11, then AB =

(A)   2   (B)   13
(C)   24   (D)   145

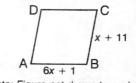

Note: Figure not drawn to scale.

2. If the diagonals of a parallelogram are perpendicular but *not* congruent, then the parallelogram is a

(A)   trapezoid   (B)   rectangle
(C)   rhombus   (D)   square

3. In parallelogram ABCD, if m∠B = 60°, then m∠C =

(A)   30°   (B)   60°
(C)   120°   (D)   300°

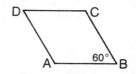

Note: Figure not drawn to scale.

4. The lengths of the sides of △LMN are 5, 6, and 7. If △ABC ~ △LMN and the shortest side of △ABC is 15, then the length of the *longest* side of △ABC is

(A) $10\frac{5}{7}$ (B) $12\frac{1}{2}$ (C)   18   (D)   21

5. If the sum of the lengths of the sides of a regular hexagon is represented by $(y - 120)$, express the length of one side of the hexagon in terms of y.

(A) $\frac{y}{5} - 24$ (B) $\frac{y}{6} - 20$

(C) $\frac{y}{8} - 15$ (D) $\frac{y}{12} - 10$

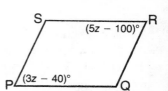

$P = y - 120$

6. A tree 10 m tall casts a shadow 25 m long. At the same time, a person casts a shadow 5 m long. The height of the person in meters is

(A)   2   (B)   12.5   (C)   50
(D)   It cannot be determined from the information given.

7. Which polygon is *not* a quadrilateral?

(A)   square   (B)   rectangle
(C)   hexagon   (D)   trapezoid

8. In parallelogram PQRS, if m∠P = (3z − 40)° and m∠R = (5z − 100)°, then m∠Q =

(A)   30°   (B)   50°
(C)   130°   (D)   150°

Note: Figure not drawn to scale.

9. What is the sum of the measures of the angles of an octagon?

(A) 540° (B) 720° (C) 1080° (D) 1440°

10. What is the name of the polygon with the sum of the measures of its angles equal to 1440°?

(A) hexagon
(C) decagon

(B) octagon
(D) dodecagon

11. In rectangle ABCD, diagonals $\overline{AC}$ and $\overline{BD}$ meet at E. If the length of AE = 5x − 7 and the length of CE = 2x + 5, then the length of $\overline{BD}$ is

(A) 4
(C) 13

(B) 11
(D) 26

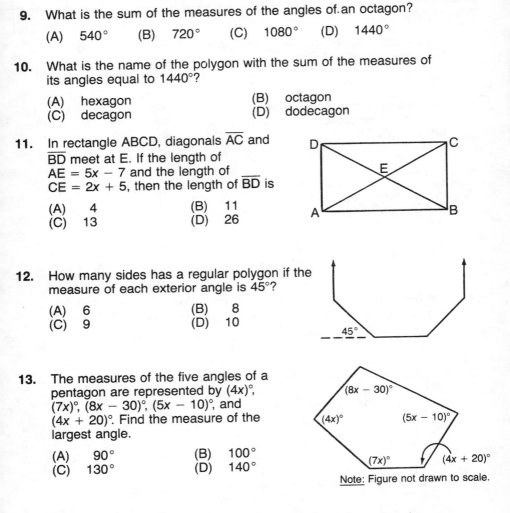

12. How many sides has a regular polygon if the measure of each exterior angle is 45°?

(A) 6
(C) 9

(B) 8
(D) 10

45°

13. The measures of the five angles of a pentagon are represented by $(4x)°$, $(7x)°$, $(8x − 30)°$, $(5x − 10)°$, and $(4x + 20)°$. Find the measure of the largest angle.

(A) 90°
(C) 130°

(B) 100°
(D) 140°

$(8x − 30)°$

$(4x)°$ $(5x − 10)°$

$(7x)°$ $(4x + 20)°$

Note: Figure not drawn to scale.

14. If the measure of an exterior angle of a regular polygon is twice the measure of an angle of the polygon, then the regular polygon is a

(A) triangle
(C) pentagon

(B) square
(D) hexagon

15. In the figure at the right, a + b =

(A) 30
(C) 90

(B) 45
(D) 120

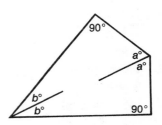

90°

$a°$
$a°$

$b°$
$b°$ 90°

TRIANGLES

1. If the length of one leg of a right triangle is 12 and the length of the hypotenuse is 13, the length of the other leg is

   (A) 1   (B) 5   (C) 25   (D) $\sqrt{313}$

2. Two angles of a triangle are equal in measure and the measure of the third angle is $140°$. The number of degrees in one of the two equal angles is

   (A) 20   (B) 40   (C) 110   (D) 160

3. In the figure at the right, if $m\angle A = 70°$ and $m\angle B = 30°$, then the measure of exterior angle BCD is

   (A) $40°$ (B) $80°$
   (C) $100°$ (D) $110°$

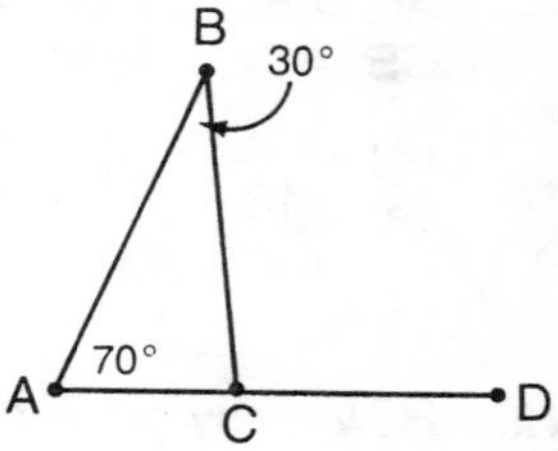

4. The measure of each base angle of an isosceles triangle is $15°$. The number of degrees in the measure of the vertex angle is

   (A) 15   (B) 60   (C) 150   (D) 165

5. In $\triangle ABC$ at the right, $\overline{CD}$ bisects $\angle ACB$ and $\overline{AE}$ bisects $\angle CAB$. If $m\angle CDE = 70°$ and $m\angle CAD = 30°$, then $m\angle B =$

   (A) $40°$ (B) $70°$
   (C) $80°$ (D) $110°$

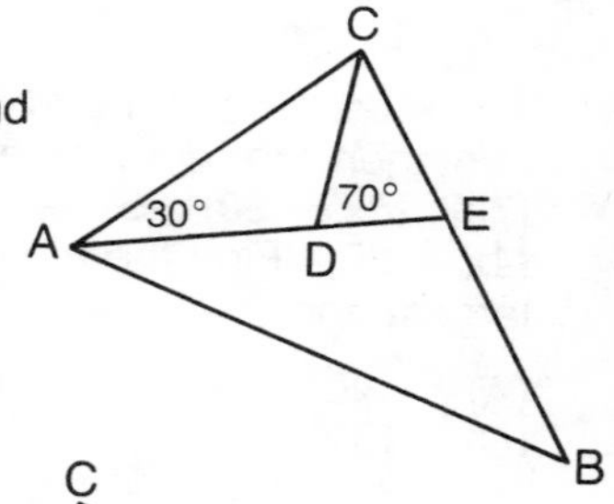

6. In right triangle ABC, $\overline{CD}$ is the altitude to the hypotenuse. If AD = 3 and CD = 4, then AC =

   (A) 1   (B) 5
   (C) $\sqrt{7}$ (D) 25

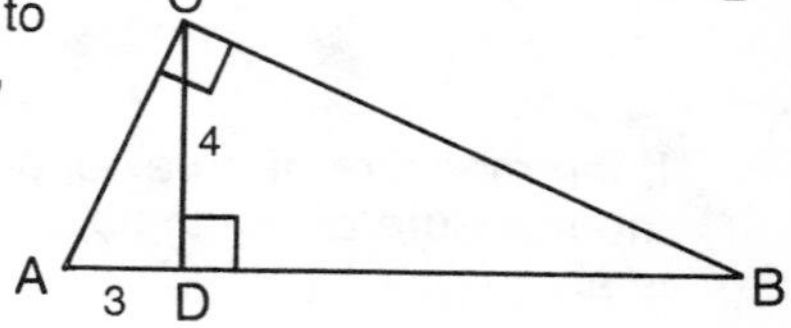

7. The length of a side of a square is $3\sqrt{2}$. What is the length of a diagonal of the square?

   (A) 3   (B) $3\sqrt{2}$
   (C) 6   (D) $6\sqrt{2}$

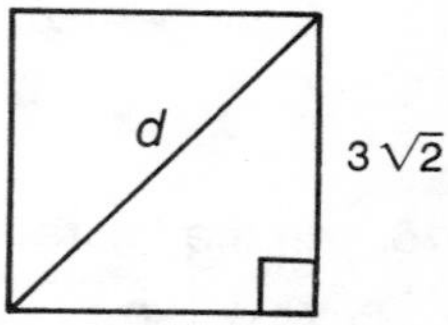

8. Which set of numbers may represent the lengths of the sides of a triangle?

   (A) {3, 5, 9}   (B) {11, 8, 3}
   (C) {5, 6, 7}   (D) {7, 1, 8}

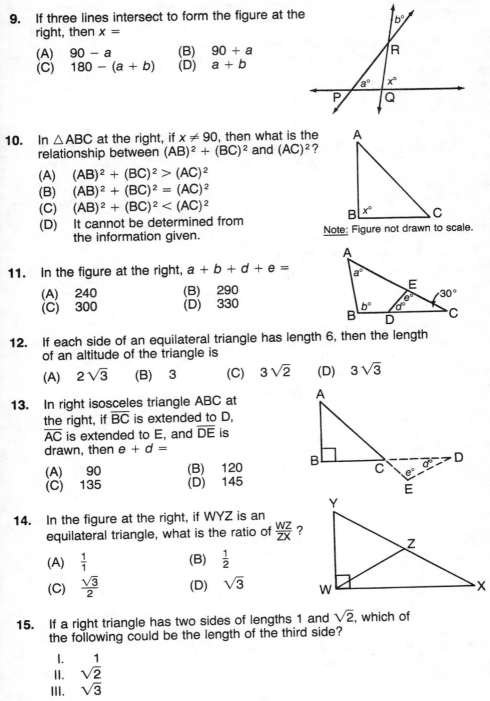

9. If three lines intersect to form the figure at the right, then $x =$

(A) $90 - a$ (B) $90 + a$
(C) $180 - (a + b)$ (D) $a + b$

10. In $\triangle ABC$ at the right, if $x \neq 90$, then what is the relationship between $(AB)^2 + (BC)^2$ and $(AC)^2$?

(A) $(AB)^2 + (BC)^2 > (AC)^2$
(B) $(AB)^2 + (BC)^2 = (AC)^2$
(C) $(AB)^2 + (BC)^2 < (AC)^2$
(D) It cannot be determined from the information given.

Note: Figure not drawn to scale.

11. In the figure at the right, $a + b + d + e =$

(A) 240   (B) 290
(C) 300   (D) 330

12. If each side of an equilateral triangle has length 6, then the length of an altitude of the triangle is

(A) $2\sqrt{3}$ (B) 3 (C) $3\sqrt{2}$ (D) $3\sqrt{3}$

13. In right isosceles triangle ABC at the right, if $\overline{BC}$ is extended to D, $\overline{AC}$ is extended to E, and $\overline{DE}$ is drawn, then $e + d =$

(A) 90   (B) 120
(C) 135   (D) 145

14. In the figure at the right, if WYZ is an equilateral triangle, what is the ratio of $\frac{WZ}{ZX}$?

(A) $\frac{1}{1}$ (B) $\frac{1}{2}$

(C) $\frac{\sqrt{3}}{2}$ (D) $\sqrt{3}$

15. If a right triangle has two sides of lengths 1 and $\sqrt{2}$, which of the following could be the length of the third side?

   I. 1
   II. $\sqrt{2}$
   III. $\sqrt{3}$

(A) I only   (B) II only
(C) III only   (D) I and III only

CIRCLES

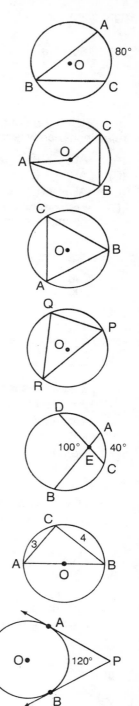

1. In the figure at the right, ∠ABC is inscribed in circle O and m$\widehat{AC}$ = 80°. The number of degrees in ∠ABC is

    (A)   20   (B)   40
    (C)   80   (D)   160

2. In the figure at the right, ∠ABC is inscribed in circle O. What is m∠ABC : m∠AOC?

    (A)   1 : 1   (B)   1 : 3
    (C)   1 : 2   (D)   2 : 1

3. If equilateral triangle ABC is inscribed in circle O as shown on the right, then m$\widehat{AB}$ =

    (A)   30°   (B)   60°
    (C)   100°   (D)   120°

4. △PQR is inscribed in circle O as shown on the right. If the ratio of m$\widehat{PQ}$: m$\widehat{QR}$: m$\widehat{RP}$ = 2 : 3 : 4, then m∠PQR =

    (A)   40°   (B)   80°
    (C)   120°   (D)   160°

5. In the figure at the right, chords AB and CD intersect at E. If m$\widehat{AC}$ = 40° and m∠DEB = 100°, then m$\widehat{BD}$ =

    (A)   100°   (B)   160°
    (C)   200°   (D)   240°

6. In the figure at the right, △ABC is inscribed in circle O. If AC = 3 and CB = 4, then the length of the radius of the circle is

    (A) $2\frac{1}{2}$ (B)   5
    (C)   7   (D) $3\frac{1}{2}$

7. In the figure at the right, tangents $\overrightarrow{PA}$ and $\overrightarrow{PB}$ are drawn to circle O. If m$\widehat{AB}$ = 120°, then m∠P =

    (A)   30°   (B)   60°
    (C)   120°   (D)   180°

8. In the figure at the right, quadrilateral ABCD is inscribed in the circle. Which angle is congruent to ∠DBC?

(A) ∠BAC   (B) ∠CDB
(C) ∠CAD   (D) ∠DEC

9. In the figure at the right, O is the center of the circle. If m∠ABC = 25°, and $\overline{AD}$ is tangent to the circle at point A, then m∠ADO =

(A) $12\frac{1}{2}°$ (B) 25°
(C) 40°   (D) 50°

10. In the figure at the right, $\overline{BC}$ is tangent to circle O at B. If OB = 1 and m∠COB = 60°, then AC =

(A) $\sqrt{3}$ (B) 2
(C) 1   (D) $2 - \sqrt{3}$

11. In the figure at the right, point O is the common center for arcs AB and CD. If m∠O = 45° and OC = 2 (OA), then m$\overarc{CD}$ − m$\overarc{AB}$ =

(A) 0°   (B) 30°
(C) 45°   (D) 90°

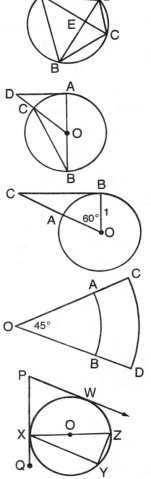

Questions 12-13 refer to the figure at the right.

12. The measure of ∠XYZ is equal to

(A) 45°   (B) m∠OXP
(C) 135°   (D) 180°

13. Angle XZY is congruent to

(A) ∠XPW   (B) ∠ZXY   (C) ∠XYZ   (D) ∠QXY

Questions 14-15 refer to the figure at the right.

14. What is the relationship between m∠ADC and m∠ABC?

(A) m∠ADC < m∠ABC
(B) m∠ADC = m∠ABC
(C) m∠ADC > m∠ABC
(D) m∠ADC + m∠ABC = 180°

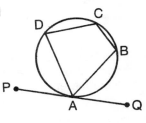

15. If m∠BAQ = 60° and m$\overarc{BC}$ = 30°, then m∠ADC =

(A) 15°   (B) 60°   (C) 75°   (D) 90°

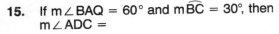

PERIMETER

1. If $\frac{3}{8}$ of the perimeter of an equilateral triangle is 6, what is the length of one side?

   (A) $2\frac{1}{4}$ (B) $5\frac{1}{3}$ (C) 4   (D) 16

2. If the side of an equilateral triangle is represented by $(x + 3)$ and the perimeter is 24, then the length of a side of the triangle is

   (A) 5   (B) 7   (C) 8   (D) 10

3. If the radius of a circle is tripled, then the circumference is

   (A) multiplied by 9   (B) cubed
   (C) increased by 3   (D) tripled

4. In the figure at the right, if the perimeter of pentagon ABCDE is $8 + 2\sqrt{2}$, then $x =$

   (A) 2   (B) $\frac{8 + 2\sqrt{2}}{5\sqrt{2}}$

   (C) $\frac{4 + \sqrt{2}}{2 + \sqrt{2}}$ (D) $\frac{4 + \sqrt{2}}{2}$

5. If the length of a diagonal of a square is $5\sqrt{2}$, then the perimeter of the square is

   (A) 5   (B) $10\sqrt{2}$
   (C) 20   (D) 25

6. In the figure at the right, ABC is an equilateral triangle and ADEF is a rhombus. If F is the midpoint of $\overline{AC}$, and the perimeter of $\triangle ABC$ is 18, then the perimeter of ADEF is

   (A) 6   (B) 12
   (C) 18   (D) 24

7. If the length of the hypotenuse of a right triangle is 6 and the length of a leg is 3, then the perimeter is

   (A) 12   (B) $9 + 3\sqrt{3}$
   (C) $9 + 3\sqrt{2}$ (D) $12\sqrt{3}$

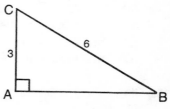

8. If the diagonals of a rhombus have lengths of 18 and 24, then the perimeter of the rhombus is

(A)   15   (B)   42   (C)   60   (D)   216

9. In the figure at the right, WZ = a and ZY = 3a. What percent of the perimeter of the rectangle is the sum WZ + ZY + YX?

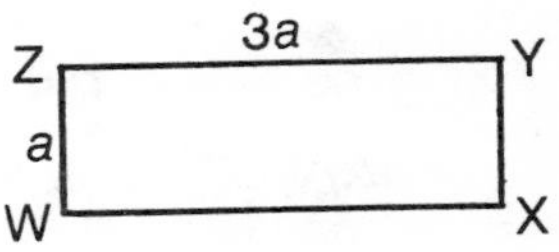

(A)   50%   (B) $62\frac{1}{2}$%

(C)   75%   (D) $87\frac{1}{2}$%

10. The lengths of the sides of a triangle are 6, 8, and 12. If the length of the shortest side of a similar triangle is 15, what is the perimeter of the larger triangle?

(A)   20   (B)   30   (C) $48\frac{3}{4}$ (D)   65

11. In the equilateral triangle DEF, DE = 10. Find the perimeter of the triangle formed by connecting the midpoints of the sides of △DEF.

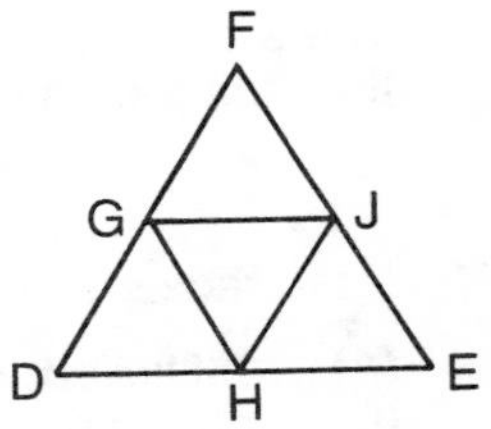

(A)   15   (B)   20
(C)   25   (D)   30

12. The measure of the length of a rectangle is 2 less than 5 times the measure of the width. If the perimeter of the rectangle is 32, the measure of the length is

(A)   3   (B)   9   (C)   13   (D) $26\frac{1}{3}$

13. In the figure at the right, $\overline{PA}$ and $\overline{PB}$ are tangents to circle O at A and B respectively. If PA = 12 and OA = 5, the perimeter of quadrilateral BPAO is

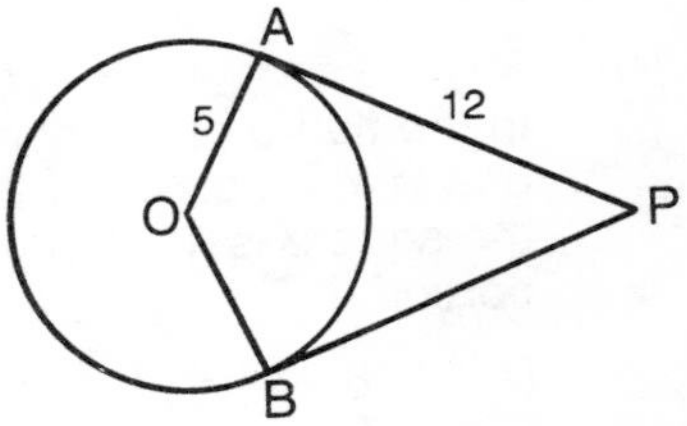

(A)   17   (B)   34
(C)   30   (D)   35

14. In the figure at the right, circle O is inscribed in △ABC. If AB = 7, AE = 3, and DC = 2, the perimeter of △ABC is

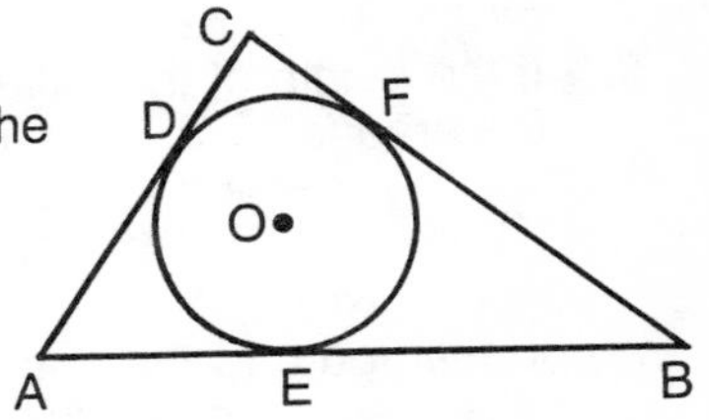

(A)   9   (B)   12
(C)   18   (D)   24

15. What is the radius of a circle with circumference 1?

(A) $\frac{1}{\pi}$ (B) $\frac{1}{2}$

(C) $1 - 2\pi$ (D) $\frac{1}{2}\pi$

AREA

1. The diameter of a circle is 8. The area of the circle is

    (A) 8π (B) 16π (C) 16   (D) 64π

2. The area of a rhombus whose diagonals have lengths 6 and 9 is

    (A) 27   (B) 24   (C) $13\frac{1}{2}$ (D) 54

3. In the figure at the right, ABCD is a trapezoid with $\overline{AB} \parallel \overline{CD}$ and altitude $\overline{DE}$. If CD = 7, DE = 4, and AB = 12, the area of ABCD is

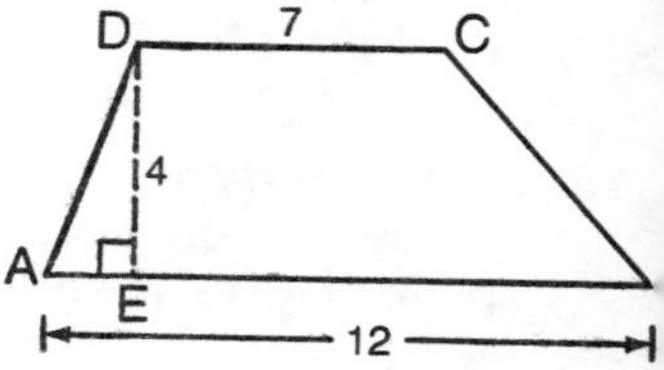

    (A) 23   (B) 38
    (C) 76   (D) 336

4. The area of a triangle is 48. If the length of the base is 16, then the length of the altitude drawn to this base is

    (A) 3   (B) 6   (C) 7   (D) 12

5. If the radius of a circle is tripled, then the area is

    (A) multiplied by 9   (B) cubed
    (C) increased by 3   (D) tripled

6. In a circle, an arc measures 120°. If the length of the arc is 8π, the area of the circle is

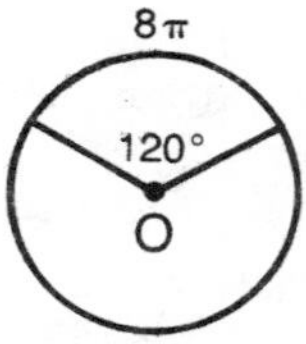

    (A) 16π (B) 24π
    (C) 144   (D) 144π

7. In the figure at the right, two semicircles are drawn in a square. If the length of the side of the square is 4, then the area of the shaded portion is

    (A) $8 - 4\pi$ (B) $8 - 2\pi$
    (C) $16 - 4\pi$ (D) $16 - 2\pi$

8. If the length of the altitude in an equilateral triangle is $3\sqrt{3}$, the area is

    (A) $9\sqrt{3}$ (B) 9   (C) $27\sqrt{3}$ (D) 6

9. In the figure at the right, the bases of isosceles trapezoid ABCD are 8 and 12. If the measure of angle A is 45°, the area of ABCD is

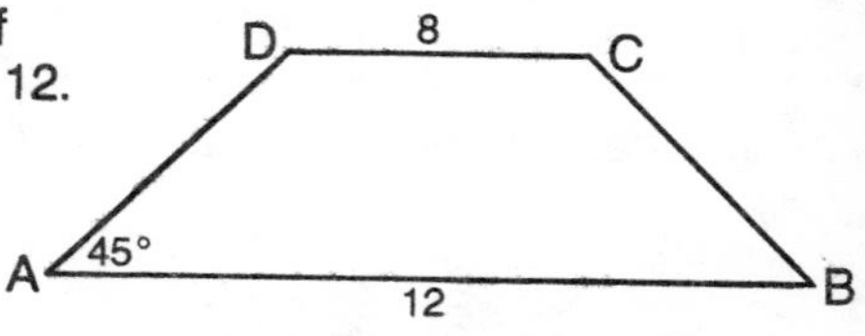

    (A) $10\sqrt{2}$ (B) 20
    (C) 40   (D) 80

10. The number of square centimeters in the total surface area of the rectangular prism shown at the right is

(A) 48   (B) 56
(C) 80   (D) 88

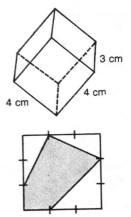

3 cm

4 cm

4 cm

11. In the figure at the right, each of the sides of the square is divided into three equal segments. $\dfrac{\text{Area of shaded region}}{\text{Area of square}} =$

(A) $\dfrac{4}{9}$ (B) $\dfrac{1}{2}$

(C) $\dfrac{8}{9}$ (D) $\dfrac{5}{9}$

12. If the perimeter of square X is triple that of square Y, then the area of X is how many times the area of Y?

(A) $\dfrac{1}{9}$ (B) 3   (C) 6   (D) 9

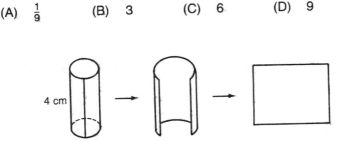

4 cm

13. The figure above shows how a cylindrical tube is opened to form a rectangular figure. If the area of the circular base is $\dfrac{9}{\pi}$ cm², then the length of the rectangle is

(A) 6π cm   (B) 6 cm   (C) $\dfrac{6}{\pi}$ cm   (D) $\dfrac{4}{\pi}$ cm

14. In the figure at the right, which of the following conditions will insure that the area of $\triangle QPR$ is equal to the area of $\triangle PSR$?

(A) $\overline{PQ} \cong \overline{RS}$ (B) $\overline{PS} \cong \overline{QR}$
(C) $m \angle PQR = m \angle PSR$ (D) $\overline{QS} \parallel \overline{PR}$

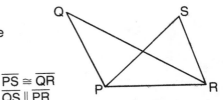

Note: Figure not drawn to scale.

15. In the figure at the right, $\triangle ABC$ has an area of 9 square meters. What is the area of the semicircle?

(A) 9πm²   (B) 18m²   (C) $\dfrac{25}{2}\pi$m²
(D) It cannot be determined from the information given.

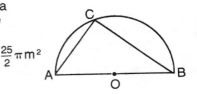

VOLUME

1. What is the volume of a rectangular prism with length 5, width 2, and height 3?

   (A)　10　　　(B)　30　　　(C)　62　　　(D)　150

2. If the total surface area of a cube is $6x^2$, the volume is

   (A)　x^2　　　(B)　$4x^2$　　　(C)　x^3　　　(D)　$6x^3$

3. The volume of a cube is 125. The sum of the lengths of all the edges is

   (A)　5　　　(B)　40　　　(C)　60　　　(D)　150

4. The volume of a right circular cylinder whose radius is 4 and whose height is one half the diameter is

   (A)　16π　　　(B)　32π　　　(C)　48π　　　(D)　64π

5. A sphere has a radius of 6. The volume is

   (A)　12　　　(B)　144π　　　(C)　216π　　　(D)　288π

6. Doubling the radius of the base of a right circular cone multiplies the volume by

   (A)　1　　　(B)　2　　　(C)　4　　　(D)　8

7. Which of the following figures could be folded along the dotted lines to form a closed rectangular prism with no overlap?

   (A)

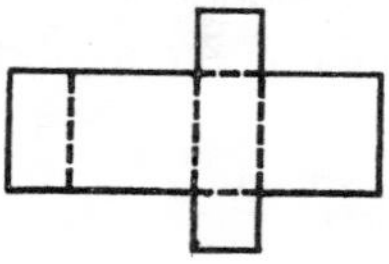

   (B)

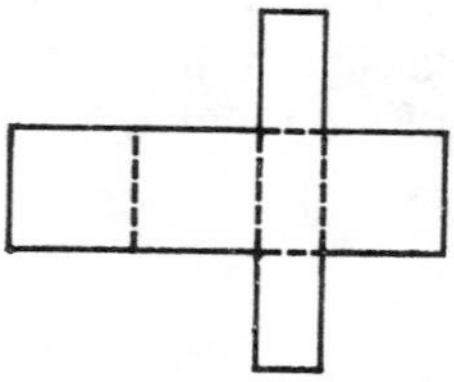

   (C)

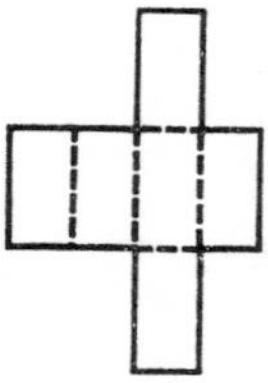

   (D)

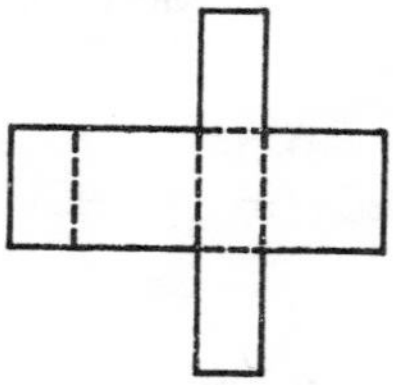

8. The following are dimensions of two right circular cylinders. All have the same volume EXCEPT the one that has

   (A)　$r = 2$　and　$h = 9$　　　(B)　$r = 3$　and　$h = 8$
   (C)　$r = 6$　and　$h = 2$　　　(D)　$r = 4$　and　$h = 4.5$

9. In the figure at the right, if an edge of each small cube has length $\frac{1}{2}$, then the volume of the entire rectangular solid is

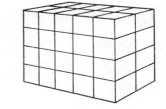

(A)   5   (B)   40
(C)   320   (D) $\frac{1}{8}$

10. The volume of a cube with edge $\sqrt{3}$ is how many times the volume of a cube with edge $\sqrt[3]{3}$?

(A) $\sqrt[3]{3}$ (B) $\sqrt{3}$ (C)   3   (D) $3\sqrt{3}$

11. Container X, of volume x, is one third full. Container Y, of volume y, is one quarter full. Container Z, of volume z, is empty. If all the fluid in the containers is divided equally among the three containers, what part of Container Z will be full?

(A) $\frac{4x + 3y}{36z}$ (B) $\frac{x + y}{3z}$ (C) $\frac{4x + 3y}{12z}$ (D) $\frac{7xy}{36z}$

12. In the figures at the right, solids A and B are halves of different rectangular prisms. How does the volume of A, V_A, compare to the volume of B, V_B?

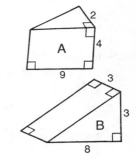

(A) $V_A > V_B$
(B) $V_A = V_B$
(C) $V_A < V_B$
(D)   It cannot be determined from the information given.

13. In a set of 36 cubic blocks, each block has pictures on 4 faces and letters on the remaining faces. How many faces of the entire set have letters?

(A)   24   (B)   72   (C)   144   (D)   216

14. If the height of the cylinder at the right is h, where $h > 1$, and the diameter is $h - 1$, then the radius of the largest sphere that will fit completely inside the cylinder is

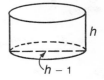

(A) $h - 1$ (B) $\frac{h}{2}$

(C) h (D) $\frac{h - 1}{2}$

15. Each of two dice is marked with a different integer from 1 to 6 inclusive. If the two dice are rolled, how many different sums of the faces up are possible?

(A)   11   (B)   12   (C)   34   (D)   36

COORDINATE GEOMETRY

1. In the figure at the right, points X(1, 2) and Y are on a straight line that passes through the origin. If A is (3, 0), what are the coordinates of B?

   (A)   (6, 0)   (B)   (0, 6)
   (C)   (0, 3)   (D)   (3, 6)

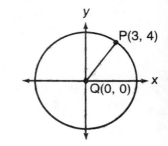

2. Point A(4, 0) is equidistant from points B and C. If the coordinates of C are (4, 4), the coordinates of B may be

   (A)   (4, −4)   (B)   (−4, −4)
   (C)   (−4, 4)   (D)   (4, 4)

3. The equation of the straight line which passes through point (0, 0) and has a slope of $-\frac{2}{3}$ is

   (A) $2y - 3x = 0$ (B) $2y + 3x = 0$
   (C) $3y + 2x = 0$ (D) $3y - 2x = 0$

4. In $\triangle ABC$, the coordinates of the vertices are A(1, 2), B(6, 1), and C(4, 5). If $\overline{AM}$ is the median drawn from A to $\overline{BC}$, the coordinates of M are

   (A) $\left(3\frac{1}{2}, 1\frac{1}{2}\right)$ (B) (5, 3)   (C) (10, 6)   (D) $\left(2\frac{1}{2}, 3\frac{1}{2}\right)$

5. The equation of the line parallel to the x-axis and four units below it is

   (A) $y = 4$ (B) $x = -4$ (C) $y = -4$ (D) $x = 4$

6. In the figure at the right, the coordinates of point P are (3, 4). If $\overline{QP}$ is a radius of a circle with center (0, 0), what is the equation of the circle?

   (A) $x + y = 5$ (B) $x^2 + y^2 = 25$
   (C) $x^2 + y^2 = 9$ (D) $x^2 + y^2 = 16$

7. The length of a line segment whose endpoints have coordinates (−1, 1) and (2, 3) is

   (A)   5   (B) $\sqrt{13}$ (C) $\sqrt{5}$ (D)   13

8. The equation of the straight line which passes through points (2, 7) and (8, −1) is

   (A) $4x + 3y = 15$ (B) $4x + 3y = 13$
   (C) $4x + 3y = 19$ (D) $4x + 3y = 29$

9. In parallelogram ABCD, the coordinates of three of the vertices are A(-1, -2), B(5, -2), and C(7, 3). The coordinates of point D are

(A) (1, 3)   (B) (-1, 3)   (C) (5, 3)   (D) (13, 3)

10. In the figure at the right, a circle with center P has an area of 16π square units and is tangent to the x- and y-axes. The coordinates of P are

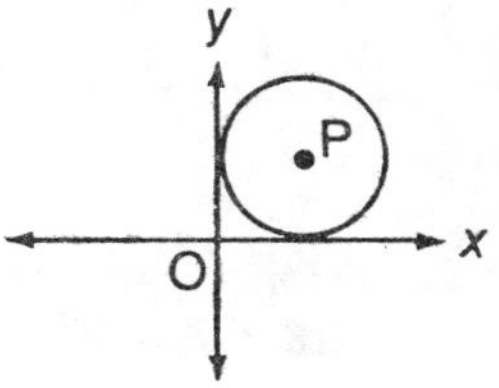

(A) (2, 8)   (B) (8, 2)
(C) (4, 4)   (D) (2, 2)

11. In the figure at the right, if $\triangle OBC$ has an area of 10, then $a =$

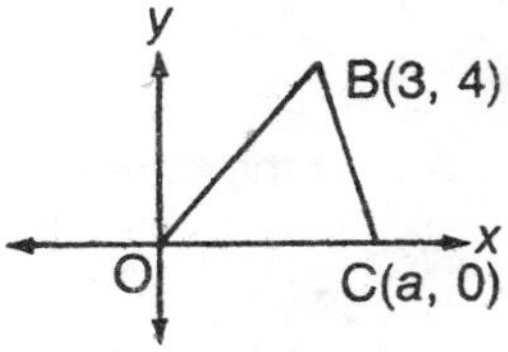

(A) 10   (B) 5

(C) $6\frac{2}{3}$ (D) $1\frac{1}{4}$ Note: Figure not drawn to scale.

12. The coordinates of points W, X, and Y are shown in the figure at the right. If $WX = YZ$ and $\overline{WX} \perp \overline{YZ}$, then the coordinates of Z are

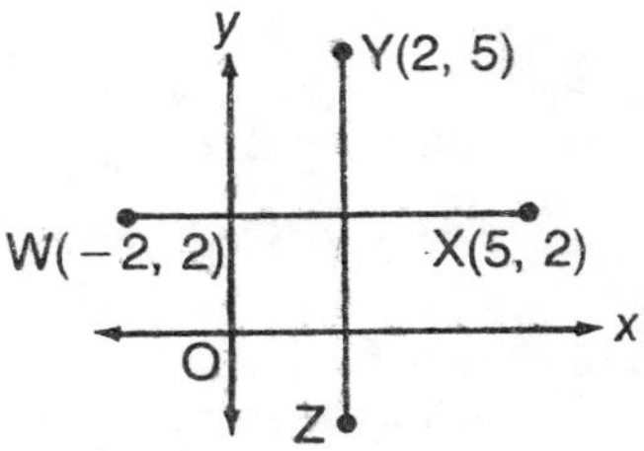

(A) (2, 0)   (B) (2, -1)
(C) (2, -2)   (D) (2, -3)

13. What is the slope of any line perpendicular to the line whose equation is $3y + 2x = 12$?

(A) $\frac{3}{2}$ (B) $-\frac{2}{3}$ (C) $\frac{2}{3}$ (D) $-\frac{3}{2}$

14. In the figure at the right, find the coordinates of R if the coordinates of P are (2, 0) and $m\angle ROP = 60°$.

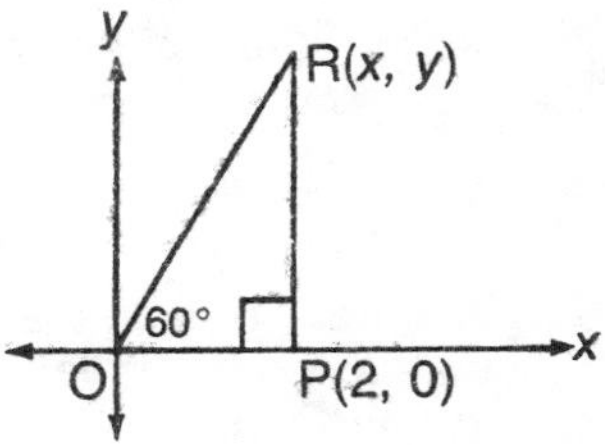

(A) (2, 2)   (B) (2, $2\sqrt{2}$)
(C) ($2\sqrt{3}$, 2)   (D) (2, $2\sqrt{3}$)

15. In the figure at the right, what is the equation of the line parallel to $\overline{AB}$ and passing through the origin?

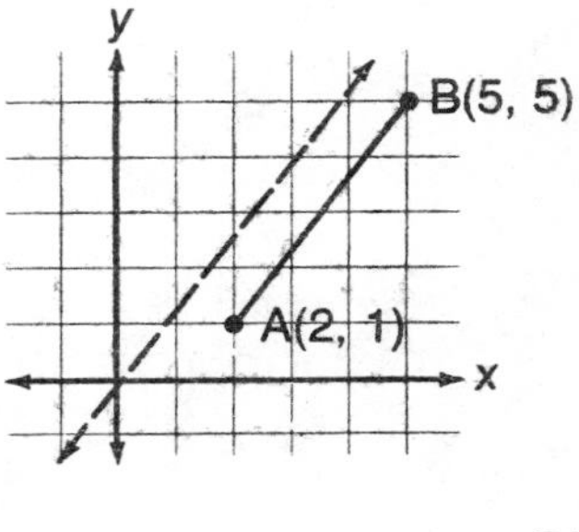

(A) $3x = 4y$ (B) $3y = -4x$
(C) $-3x = 4y$ (D) $3y = 4x$

PROBLEM SOLVING

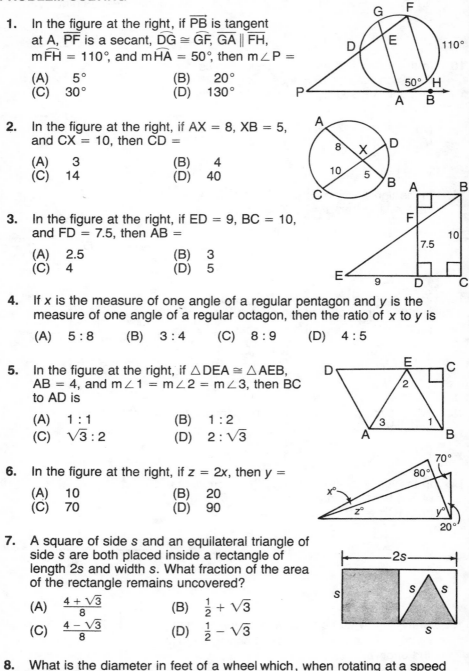

1. In the figure at the right, if $\overrightarrow{PB}$ is tangent at A, $\overline{PF}$ is a secant, $\overset{\frown}{DG} \cong \overset{\frown}{GF}$, $\overline{GA} \parallel \overline{FH}$, $m\overset{\frown}{FH} = 110°$, and $m\overset{\frown}{HA} = 50°$, then $m\angle P =$

   (A)   5°   (B)   20°
   (C)   30°   (D)   130°

2. In the figure at the right, if AX = 8, XB = 5, and CX = 10, then CD =

   (A)   3   (B)   4
   (C)   14   (D)   40

3. In the figure at the right, if ED = 9, BC = 10, and FD = 7.5, then AB =

   (A)   2.5   (B)   3
   (C)   4   (D)   5

4. If x is the measure of one angle of a regular pentagon and y is the measure of one angle of a regular octagon, then the ratio of x to y is

   (A)   5 : 8   (B)   3 : 4   (C)   8 : 9   (D)   4 : 5

5. In the figure at the right, if $\triangle DEA \cong \triangle AEB$, AB = 4, and $m\angle 1 = m\angle 2 = m\angle 3$, then BC to AD is

   (A)   1 : 1   (B)   1 : 2
   (C) $\sqrt{3}$: 2   (D)   2 : $\sqrt{3}$

6. In the figure at the right, if $z = 2x$, then $y =$

   (A)   10   (B)   20
   (C)   70   (D)   90

7. A square of side s and an equilateral triangle of side s are both placed inside a rectangle of length $2s$ and width s. What fraction of the area of the rectangle remains uncovered?

   (A) $\dfrac{4 + \sqrt{3}}{8}$ (B) $\dfrac{1}{2} + \sqrt{3}$

   (C) $\dfrac{4 - \sqrt{3}}{8}$ (D) $\dfrac{1}{2} - \sqrt{3}$

8. What is the diameter in feet of a wheel which, when rotating at a speed of 10 revolutions per minute, takes 18 seconds to travel 15 feet?

   (A) $\dfrac{5}{\pi}$ (B) $\dfrac{15}{\pi}$ (C) 5π (D) $\dfrac{5}{2\pi}$

9. In △ABC at the right, D and E are points on $\overline{AB}$ and $\overline{BC}$ respectively, so that $\overline{DE} \parallel \overline{AC}$. If F is a point on $\overline{AC}$, what is the ratio of the area of △DEF to that of trapezoid DECA?

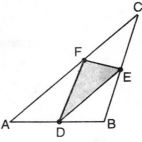

(A) 1 : 2   (B) 1 : 3   (C) 1 : 4

(D) It cannot be determined from the information given.

10. In rectangle ABCD at the right, point E is closer to side $\overline{AB}$ than to side $\overline{CD}$. If E moves towards side $\overline{CD}$, the area covered by the shaded part will

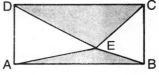

(A) increase
(B) decrease
(C) decrease, then increase
(D) remain the same

11. In the two rectangles at the right, what is AB + CD?

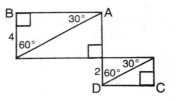

(A) $6\sqrt{2}$ (B) $6\sqrt{3}$

(C) $6\sqrt{6}$ (D) 18

12. A jeweler can bend a piece of wire to make a circle with a radius of 14 cm. How large an area could she enclose with the same piece of wire if she made a square instead? (Use $\pi \approx \frac{22}{7}$.)

(A) 49π cm²   (B) 196π cm²
(C) 88 cm²   (D) 484 cm²

13. On a graph, point A is located at (0, 6). Point B is located 8 units below point A along the y-axis and 2 units to the left on a line parallel to the x-axis. What is the length of AB?

(A) $\sqrt{60}$ (B) $\sqrt{66}$ (C) $\sqrt{68}$ (D) 68

14. In the figure at the right, AOB and COD are sectors of circles with center O. If OD = 2, OB = 4, and m∠O = 30°, what is the area of the shaded region?

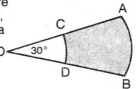

(A) $\frac{\pi}{3}$ (B) $\frac{2}{3}\pi$

(C) π (D) $\frac{4}{3}\pi$

15. If each angle of a quadrilateral measures less than 120° and if three of its angles each measure $x°$, which of the following must be true?

(A) $x > 80$ (B) $x = 80$
(C) $x < 80$ (D) The quadrilateral is a square.

Answer Key To Practice Tests

Following each answer, there is a number or numbers in the form "*a.b*" in parentheses. This number refers to the Geometry Refresher (beginning on page 23). The first number "*a*" indicates the Math section:

1. Angles	6. Perimeter
2. Lines	7. Area
3. Polygons	8. Volume
4. Triangles	9. Coordinate Geometry
5. Circles	10. Problem Solving

The number "*b*" indicates the part of the section that explains the rule or method used in solving the problem.

ANGLES

1. C (1.5)	**9.** C (1.2, 1.6)
2. D (1.2)	**10.** B (1.5, 1.4)
3. A (1.7)	**11.** B (1.9, 1.5)
4. D (1.5)	**12.** D (1.6, 1.2)
5. B (1.5, 1.9)	**13.** A (1.8)
6. D (1.6, 1.5)	**14.** D (1.7, 1.8)
7. A (1.9)	**15.** A (1.8)
8. D (1.4, 1.3)	

LINES

1. B (2.4)	**9.** A (2.6, 1.8)
2. C (2.4, 1.3, 1.6)	**10.** C (2.6)
3. B (2.6)	**11.** D (2.1)
4. B (2.1)	**12.** A (2.6)
5. B (2.6)	**13.** B (2.5)
6. D (2.4)	**14.** C (2.4)
7. D (2.8)	**15.** D (2.6, 1.8)
8. B (2.3)	

POLYGONS

1. B (3.6)	**9.** C (3.3, 3.2)
2. C (3.6)	**10.** C (3.3, 3.2)
3. C (3.6, 1.8)	**11.** D (3.6)
4. D (3.5)	**12.** B (3.3)
5. B (3.2)	**13.** D (3.3)
6. A (3.5)	**14.** A (3.3, 3.2, 3.1)
7. C (3.6, 3.2)	**15.** C (3.3)
8. C (3.6, 1.8)	

TRIANGLES

1. B (4.8)	**9.** D (4.6, 1.9)
2. A (4.3)	**10.** D (4.8)
3. C (4.6)	**11.** C (4.3)
4. C (4.5, 4.3)	**12.** D (4.2, 4.8)
5. A (4.6, 4.2, 4.3)	**13.** C (4.8, 1.9, 4.3)
6. B (4.2, 4.8)	**14.** A (4.3, 4.5)
7. C (4.8)	**15.** D (4.8)
8. C (4.7)	

CIRCLES

1. B (5.7)	**9.** C (5.1, 4.6, 5.4)
2. C (5.7, 5.6)	**10.** C (5.4, 4.8)
3. D (5.7, 4.3)	**11.** A (5.6)
4. B (5.5, 5.7)	**12.** B (5.7, 5.4)
5. B (5.8)	**13.** D (5.7, 5.8)
6. A (5.1, 5.7, 4.8)	**14.** D (5.7)
7. B (5.8, 5.5)	**15.** C (5.8, 5.7)
8. C (5.7, 1.3)	

PERIMETER

1. B (6.2)	**9.** B (6.3)
2. C (6.2)	**10.** D (6.2, 3.5)
3. D (6.4)	**11.** A (6.2, 2.3, 4.4)
4. A (6.1, 4.8)	**12.** C (6.3)
5. C (6.3, 4.8)	**13.** B (6.1, 5.4, 5.1)
6. B (6.2, 2.3, 6.1)	**14.** C (6.2, 5.4)
7. B (6.2, 4.8)	**15.** D (6.4)
8. C (6.1, 3.6, 4.8)	

AREA

1. B (7.6, 5.1)
2. A (7.3)
3. B (7.4)
4. B (7.5)
5. A (7.6)
6. D (7.6, 5.6, 6.4)
7. C (7.1, 7.6)
8. A (7.5, 4.8)
9. B (7.4, 3.6)
10. C (7.8)
11. D (7.1, 7.5)
12. D (7.1, 6.3)
13. B (7.6, 6.4)
14. D (7.5, 2.5)
15. D (7.5, 7.6, 4.8)

VOLUME

1. B (8.1)
2. C (8.1, 7.8)
3. C (8.1, 7.8)
4. D (8.2)
5. D (8.2)
6. C (8.2)
7. D (8.1, 7.8)
8. A (8.2)
9. A (8.1)
10. B (8.1)
11. A (8.1)
12. B (8.1)
13. B (8.1, 7.8)
14. D (8.2)
15. A (8.1, 7.8)

COORDINATE GEOMETRY

1. B (9.10, 9.6, 9.5)
2. A (9.9, 9.6, 9.5)
3. C (9.12)
4. B (9.9, 4.2)
5. C (9.11, 9.10)
6. B (9.8, 9.7)
7. B (9.7)
8. D (9.12)
9. A (9.7, 3.6)
10. C (9.5, 7.6)
11. B (9.5, 7.5)
12. C (9.7, 9.5)
13. A (9.11, 9.12)
14. D (9.7, 4.8)
15. D (9.11, 9.12)

PROBLEM SOLVING

1. C (5.8, 5.5)
2. C (3.5, 5.7)
3. B (3.5, 1.9, 2.6)
4. D (10.3, 3.3)
5. C (4.3, 4.4, 4.8)
6. C (4.3)
7. C (7.1, 7.5)
8. A (10.6, 6.4)
9. D (7.5, 7.4)
10. D (7.5)
11. B (4.8)
12. D (6.4, 7.1)
13. C (9.6, 9.7)
14. C (7.6)
15. A (3.3)

Solutions for
Geometry Practice Tests

ANGLES

1. (C) AB is a line segment which forms a straight angle. The degree
measure of a straight angle is 180.
$$x + x + x + x + x = 180$$
$$5x = 180$$
$$x = 36$$

  If your choice was
  (A), you used 90° as the measure of a straight angle.
  (B or D), see the solution above.

2. (D) Let x = the degree measure of $\angle$ B
  $3x$ = the degree measure of $\angle$ A

  Then,
$$x + 3x = 60$$
$$4x = 60$$
$$x = 15$$

  So
$$3x = 45$$

  If your choice was
  (A), you found the value of x but divided by 3 instead of
      multiplying by 3.
  (B), you found the degree measure of $\angle$ B.
  (C), you solved $x + 3x = 60$ as $2x = 60$.

3. (A) Complementary angles are two angles whose sum is 90°.
  Thus,
$$(3x - 10)° + (2x + 10)° = 90°$$
$$3x - 10 + 2x + 10 = 90$$
$$5x = 90$$
$$x = 18$$

  If your choice was
  (B), you solved the equation as $5x = 110$.
  (C), you thought the angles were equal to each other,
      $3x - 10 = 2x + 10$.
  (D), you used 180° as the sum of two complementary
      angles.

4. (D) The degree measure of a straight angle is 180, so
$$x + y + x = 180$$
$$2x + y = 180$$
$$y = 180 - 2x$$

  If your choice was
  (A, B, or C), see the solution above.

5. (B) The degree measure of a straight angle is 180, so
$$(5y - 2) + (3y + 6) = 180$$
$$8y + 4 = 180$$
$$8y = 176$$
$$y = 22$$

Since vertical angles are congruent,
$$(9r)° = (5y - 2)°$$
$$9r = 5(22) - 2$$
$$9r = 108$$
$$r = 12$$

If your choice was
(A), you considered the angle whose measure is $(9r)°$ as a right angle.
(C or D), see the solution above.

6. (D) The sum of the degree measures of all the consecutive adjacent angles about a point in the plane is 360. Thus, $a + b + c + d + e = 360$.

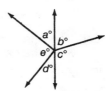

If your choice was
(A), see the solution above.
(B), you considered these angles as consecutive adjacent angles whose rays are perpendicular.
(C), you considered these angles as consecutive adjacent angles whose rays form a straight line.

7. (A) Vertical angles are congruent, so $s = y$.

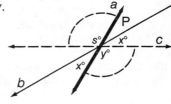

If your choice was
(B), you included both angles of $x°$ each.
(C), see the solution above.
(D), you included one angle of $x°$. See the diagram at the right.

8. (D) An angle bisector is the ray which divides the angle into two congruent angles. Therefore,
$$m∠ABD = m∠DBC$$
$$(2x + 18)° = (4x - 18)°$$
$$2x + 18 = 4x - 18$$
$$36 = 2x$$
$$18 = x$$
$$4x - 18 = 4(18) - 18 = 54°$$

If your choice was
(A), you solved $2x + 18 = 4x - 18$ as $6x = 36$.
(B), you only found the value of x, not $m∠DBC$.
(C), you did not complete the solution of $2x = 36$.

9. (C) Use this equation.

$$m \angle COD = m \angle AOD - m \angle AOC$$
$$m \angle COD = 120° - 70°$$
$$m \angle COD = 50°$$

Then, $m \angle BOC = m \angle BOD - m \angle COD$
$$m \angle BOC = 85° - 50°$$
$$m \angle BOC = 35°$$

If your choice was
(A), you found $m \angle BOC = m \angle BOD - m \angle AOC$.
(B), see the solution above.
(D), you found the measure of $\angle COD$.

10. (B) The measure of each angle as shown
in the figure at the right is 15°. The
measure of an angle that can be
formed must be a multiple of 15:
15, 30, 45, 60, 75, or 90.

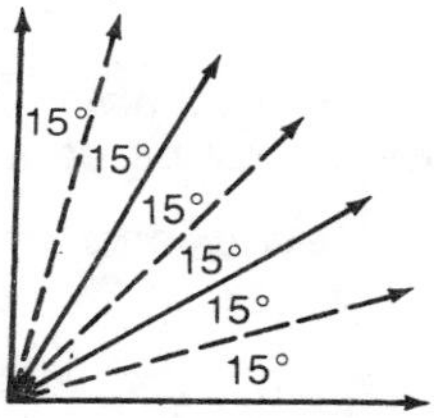

Since 40 is not a multiple of 15, it
could not be the degree measure of
any of the angles formed.

If your choice was
(A, C, or D), see the solution above.

11. (B) Since vertical angles are congruent, the measures of the two
missing angles are each $c°$. The sum of the measures of the
angles about a point is 360°, so
$$a + b + 4c = 360$$
$$a = 360 - b - 4c$$

If your choice was
(A), you used the sum of the measures of the angles about
a point as 180°.
(C or D), see the solution above.

12. (D) Use this equation.

$$m \angle CMD = m \angle AMD - m \angle AMC$$
$$m \angle CMD = 90° - 75°$$
$$m \angle CMD = 15°$$

Then, $m \angle BMD = m \angle BMC + m \angle CMD$
$$m \angle BMD = 25° + 15°$$
$$m \angle BMD = 40°$$

If your choice was
(A), you subtracted $m \angle BMC$ from $m \angle AMD$.
(B), you found $m \angle CMD$.
(C), you found $m \angle AMB$ by subtracting $m \angle BMC$ from
 $m \angle AMC$.

13. (A) The sum of the degree measures of supplementary angles ABC and ABD is 180.

Let z = the degree measure of $\angle$ ABD

Then,
$$z + 180 - y + 2x = 180$$
$$z = y - 2x$$

If your choice was
(B), you solved the equation incorrectly.
(C or D), see the solution above.

14. (D) If $\angle$ A is complementary to $\angle$ B, then $m\angle A + m\angle B = 90°$ and statement III is true. Then, multiply both sides of the equation by 2.
$$2(m\angle A + m\angle B) = 2(90°)$$
$$2m\angle A + 2m\angle B = 180°$$

Thus statement I is true. Statement II is not true since $m\angle A$ need not be equal to the $m\angle B$.

If your choice was
(A, B, or C), see the solution above.

15. (A) Supplementary angles are two angles whose sum is 180°.

Let $\quad n$ = the degree measure of the smaller angle
$6n + 40$ = the degree measure of the larger angle

Then,
$$n + 6n + 40 = 180$$
$$7n = 140$$
$$n = 20$$

If your choice was
(B), you subtracted n from $6n$ and got the equation $5n + 40 = 180$.
(C), you added 40 to one side and subtracted 40 from the other side and solved the equation $7n = 220$.
(D), you found the degree measure of the larger angle.

LINES

1. (B) If two lines are perpendicular, then the intersection of two distinct straight lines is a point.

If your choice was
(A, C, or D), see the solution above.

2. (C) If two lines intersect and form congruent adjacent angles, then they are perpendicular.

If your choice was
(A), both lines need not have equal measures.
(B), parallel lines do not intersect.
(D), both lines could not be vertical.

3. (B) If two lines are parallel and intersected by a transversal, the consecutive interior angles are supplementary.

Thus, $m\angle 1 + m\angle 2 + m\angle 3 = 180°$
$65° + 50° + m\angle 3 = 180°$
$m\angle 3 = 65°$

If your choice was
(A), you thought $m\angle 2 = m\angle 3$.
(C), you found $m\angle 2 + m\angle 3 = 115°$ but did not find $m\angle 3$.
(D), you thought that $\angle 2$ and $\angle 3$ were supplementary.

4. **(B)** Draw a diagram to picture the problem.

lines: 1   2   3   ?

points: 0   1   3   6

If your choice was
(A, C, or D), see the solution above.

5. **(B)** If two lines are parallel, the alternate interior angles are congruent. Therefore, $a = b = 65$.
Thus, $b - c = 65 - 45 = 20$.

If your choice was
(A), you thought that $b = c$.
(C), you thought that $\angle a$ and $\angle c$ were alternate interior angles and found only c.
(D), you thought that $a + b = 180$ and $b = 115$.

6. **(D)** If $n \perp m$, angles 1 and 4 must be right angles.

If your choice was
(A, B, or C), see the solution above.

7. **(D)** If two lines are parallel to the same line, the two lines are parallel to each other. Thus, $\ell_1 \parallel \ell_2$. Statement I is true.

If a line is perpendicular to one of two parallel lines, then it is perpendicular to the other line also. Thus, $\ell_2 \perp \ell_4$. It is also true that $\ell_1 \parallel \ell_3$, so that $\ell_3 \perp \ell_4$. Both statements II and III are true.

If your choice was
(A, B, or C), see the solution above.

8. **(B)** Since $BD = BC + CD$ and $BD = 18$, then $BC + CD = 18$.
If B is the midpoint of $\overline{AC}$, then $BC = AB$.
If D is the midpoint of $\overline{CE}$, then $CD = DE$.

Add the two equations. $BC + CD = AB + DE$

Since $BC + CD = 18$, then $AB + DE = 18$ and $AE = 36$.

If your choice was
(A, C, or D), see the solution above.

9. (A) Since $\overline{AB} \parallel \overline{CD}$, the alternate interior angles are congruent. Thus, $m\angle ABC = m\angle BCD = 105°$. Angle x is supplementary to $\angle ABC$, so $x = 75$.

> *If your choice was*
> (B), you found $m\angle ABC = 100°$.
> (C), you found $m\angle ABC = 95°$.
> (D), you thought $\angle x$ and $\angle BCD$ were alternate interior angles.

10. (C) Since $\ell \parallel m$, the corresponding angles are congruent, so $\angle 3 \cong \angle 4$.

> *If your choice was*
> (A), $m\angle 1 = m\angle 3$, and $m\angle 3 = m\angle 4$, so $m\angle 1 = m\angle 4$. If $m\angle 4 + m\angle 8 = 180°$, then $m\angle 1 + m\angle 8 = 180°$.
> (B), $m\angle 2 + m\angle 5 = 180°$, and $m\angle 5 = m\angle 6$, then $m\angle 2 + m\angle 6 = 180°$.
> (D), $m\angle 5 = m\angle 6$, and $m\angle 6 + m\angle 7 = 180°$, so $m\angle 5 + m\angle 7 = 180°$.

11. (D) Experiment by drawing lines in the diagram. Thus, there are 5 nonoverlapping regions.

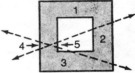

> *If your choice was*
> (A, B, or C), see the solution above.

12. (A) If $\ell_1 \parallel \ell_2$, then $x + y = 180$. If ℓ_1 rotates to the position of the dotted line, then $x + y < 180$.

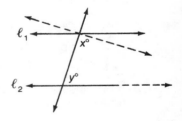

> *If your choice was*
> (B), for $x + y$ to equal 180, ℓ_1 must be parallel to ℓ_2.
> (C), the lines would have to meet when extended to the left.
> (D), see the solution above.

13. (B) The distance between parallel lines is the length of the perpendicular segment drawn from any point of one line to the other line. Since $x = y = 90$ and parallel lines are everywhere equidistant, it follows that $PQ = RS$.

> *If your choice was*
> (A), x would be greater than y.
> (C), x would be less than y.
> (D), see the solution above.

14. (C) Since $\overrightarrow{BA} \perp \overrightarrow{BC}$, $m\angle ABC = 90°$.
$$m\angle ABD + m\angle CBD = m\angle ABC$$
$$(3x - 5)° + (5x - 17)° = 90°$$
$$3x - 5 + 5x - 17 = 90$$
$$8x - 22 = 90$$
$$8x = 112$$
$$x = 14$$
$$(3x - 5)° = [3(14) - 5]° = 37°$$

If your choice was
(A), you found *x* and not m∠ABD.
(B), you added 22 to one side and subtracted 22 from the other side of the equation.
(D), you found m∠CBD.

15. (D) If two lines are parallel, the corresponding angles are congruent. Therefore, m∠1 = m∠3. Angles 2 and 3 are supplementary, therefore angles 1 and 2 are supplementary.

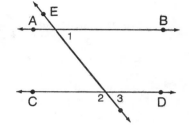

$(2x + 10)° + (3x − 20)° = 180°$
$2x + 10 + 3x − 20 = 180$
$5x − 10 = 180$
$5x = 190$
$x = 38$
$(3x − 20)° = [3(38) − 20]° = 94°$

If your choice was
(A), you believed m∠1 = m∠2.
(B), you only found the value of *x*.
(C), you found m∠1, not m∠2.

POLYGONS

1. (B) In a rhombus, the measures of all sides are equal. So
$$AB = CD$$
$$6x + 1 = x + 11$$
$$5x = 10$$
$$x = 2$$
$$6x + 1 = 6(2) + 1 = 13$$

If your choice was
(A), you only found the value of *x*, and not the length of $\overline{AB}$.
(C), you thought the two sides were supplementary and only found *x*.
(D), see (C) above and you found AB.

2. (C) In a rhombus, the diagonals are perpendicular but they are *not* congruent.

If your choice was
(A or D), the diagonals would be congruent if they are perpendicular.
(B), the diagonals would be congruent but not perpendicular.

3. (C) In a parallelogram, the consecutive angles are supplementary. Therefore, m∠B + m∠C = 180°. Thus, m∠C = 120°.

If your choice was
(A), you believed that ∠B and ∠C are complementary.
(B), you believed that ∠B ≅ ∠C because they are opposite angles.
(D), you thought the sum of two consecutive angles was 360°.

4. (D) Let x = the length of the longest side of △ABC

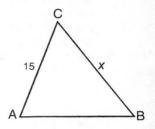

Since △LMN ~ △ABC, the longest side of △ABC corresponds to the longest side, 7, of △LMN. The shortest side of △ABC, 15, corresponds to the shortest side, 5, of △LMN.

If the triangles are similar, the corresponding sides are in proportion.

$$\frac{x}{7} = \frac{15}{5}$$
$$\frac{x}{7} = \frac{3}{1}$$
$$x = 21$$

If your choice was
(A), you used the proportion $\frac{x}{5} = \frac{15}{7}$.
(B), you used the proportion $\frac{x}{5} = \frac{15}{6}$.
(C), you found the length of the middle side.

5. (B) A regular hexagon has 6 sides of equal measure. The length of any one side is $\frac{1}{6}$ of the sum of the lengths.

$$\frac{1}{6}(y - 120) = \frac{y}{6} - \frac{120}{6}$$
$$= \frac{y}{6} - 20$$

If your choice was
(A), you thought a hexagon had 5 sides.
(C), you thought a hexagon had 8 sides.
(D), you thought a hexagon had 12 sides.

6. (A) Draw a diagram to picture the problem. Set up and solve the proportion.

$$\frac{x}{10} = \frac{5}{25}$$
$$\frac{x}{10} = \frac{1}{5}$$
$$5x = 10$$
$$x = 2$$

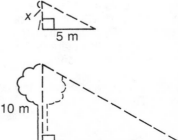

If your choice was
(B), you used the proportion $\frac{x}{25} = \frac{5}{10}$.
(C), you used the proportion $\frac{x}{10} = \frac{25}{5}$.
(D), see the solution above.

7. (C) A quadrilateral is a polygon that has 4 sides. A rectangle, a square, and a trapezoid each have 4 sides. A hexagon is a polygon that has 6 sides. Therefore, the hexagon is *not* a quadrilateral.

If your choice was
(A, B, or D), see the solution above.

8. (C) The measures of a pair of opposite angles in a parallelogram are equal, so
$$(3z - 40)° = (5z - 100)°$$
$$3z - 40 = 5z - 100$$
$$60 = 2z$$
$$30 = z$$
$$m \angle P = (3z - 40)° = [3(30) - 40]° = 50°$$

Angle Q is supplementary to $\angle P$ and $\angle R$, so
$$m \angle Q + m \angle P = 180°$$
$$m \angle Q + 50° = 180°$$
$$m \angle Q = 130°$$

If your choice was
(A), you only solved for z.
(B), you found $m \angle P$.
(D), you found the supplement of z.

9. (C) The sum of the measures of the angles of an octagon (8 sides) is $(8 - 2)180° = 6(180°) = 1080°$.

If your choice was
(A), you thought an octagon had 5 sides.
(B), you thought an octagon had 6 sides.
(D), you thought an octagon had 10 sides.

10. (C) The sum of the measures of the angles of a polygon of n sides is $(n - 2)180°$, so
$$(n - 2)180° = 1440°$$
$$n - 2 = 8$$
$$n = 10$$

If your choice was
(A, B, or D), see the solution above.

11. (D) The diagonals of a rectangle bisect each other so,
$$AE = CE$$
$$5x - 7 = 2x + 5$$
$$3x = 12$$
$$x = 4$$
$$CE = 2x + 5 = 2(4) + 5 = 13$$

The lengths of the diagonals of a rectangle are equal, so
AC = BD. Since AC = AE + CE, AC = 26 and BD = 26.

If your choice was
(A), you only solved for *x*.
(B), you found CE = 2(4) + 5 as 6 + 5 = 11.
(C), you found only the lengths of AE and CE.

12. (B) The measure of each exterior angle of a regular polygon of
n sides is $\frac{360°}{n}$.

Therefore, $\qquad\qquad\qquad\qquad \frac{360°}{n} = 45°$

$$45n = 360$$
$$n = 8$$

If your choice was
(A, C, or D), see the solution above.

13. (D) The sum of the measures of the angles of a pentagon is
$(5 - 2)180° = 3(180°) = 540°$.
Write an equation and solve.
$(4x)° + (7x)° + (8x - 30)° + (5x - 10)° + (4x + 20)° = 540°$
$$4x + 7x + 8x - 30 + 5x - 10 + 4x + 20 = 540$$
$$28x - 20 = 540$$
$$28x = 560$$
$$x = 20$$

$(4x)° = 80°; (7x)° = 140°; (8x - 30)° = 130°;$
$(5x - 10)° = 90; (4x + 20)° = 100°$
Thus, the measure of the largest angle is 140°.

If your choice was
(A), you chose $(5x - 10)°$ as the measure of the largest
angle.
(B), you chose $(4x + 20)°$ as the measure of the largest
angle.
(C), you chose $(8x - 30)°$ as the measure of the largest
angle.

14. (A) Let *n* = the measure of the interior angle
$2n$ = the measure of the exterior angle

Since the interior angle and the exterior angle of a polygon are
supplementary, then
$$n + 2n = 180°$$
$$3n = 180°$$
$$n = 60° \text{ and } 2n = 120°$$

The measure of each exterior angle of a regular polygon of
n sides is $\frac{360°}{n}$.

Therefore, $\qquad\qquad\qquad\qquad \frac{360°}{n} = 120°$
$$120n = 360$$
$$n = 3$$
Thus, a polygon having 3 sides is a triangle.

If your choice was
(B) you used the equation $2n = 180°$.
(C) you used the equation $\frac{360°}{n} = 60°$ and incorrectly solved it as $n = 5$.
(D) you used the equation $\frac{360°}{n} = 60°$.

15. (C) The sum of the measures of the angles of a quadrilateral is $360°$.
Therefore, $\quad (2a)° + (2b)° + 90° + 90° = 360°$
$$2a + 2b = 180$$
$$a + b = 90$$

If your choice was
(A, B, or D), see the solution above.

TRIANGLES

1. (B) Let x = the length of the other leg

Then use the Pythagorean theorem.
$$x^2 + 12^2 = 13^2$$
$$x^2 + 144 = 169$$
$$x^2 = 25$$
$$x = 5$$

If your choice was
(A), you forgot to square the legs and the hypotenuse.
(C), you solved for x^2 but not x.
(D), you used 12 and 13 as the legs and found the hypotenuse.

2. (A) Let x = the degree measure of one of the equal angles

Then, $\quad\quad\quad x + x + 140 = 180$
$$2x = 40$$
$$x = 20$$

If your choice was
(B), you wrote the equation as $x + 140 = 180$.
(C), you thought the sum of the measures of the angles in a triangle was $360°$.
(D), you solved $x + x + 140 = 180$ as $2x = 320$.

3. (C) The exterior angle of a triangle is equal to the sum of the measures of the nonadjacent angles of the triangle.
$$m \angle BCD = m \angle A + m \angle B$$
$$m \angle BCD = 70° + 30°$$
$$m \angle BCD = 100°$$

If your choice was
(A), you subtracted the measures.
(B), you found the measure of $\angle ACB$.
(D), you found the sum of $30°$ and $70°$ as $110°$.

4. (C) Let x = the degree measure of the vertex angle

Then,
$$x + 15 + 15 = 180$$
$$x + 30 = 180$$
$$x = 150$$

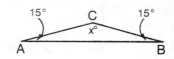

If your choice was
(A), you thought all the angles of the triangle were congruent.
(B), you thought the sum of the measures of the angles was 90°.
(D), you wrote the equation as $x + 15 = 180$.

5. (A) $\angle$ CDE is an exterior angle of $\triangle$ ACD so,
$$m\angle CDE = m\angle CAD + m\angle ACD$$
$$70° = 30° + m\angle ACD$$
$$40° = m\angle ACD$$

Since $\overline{CD}$ bisects $\angle$ ACB, $m\angle ACD = m\angle DCE = 40°$.
Therefore, $m\angle ACB = 80°$.

Since $\overline{AE}$ bisects $\angle$ CAB, $m\angle CAD = m\angle BAD = 30°$.
Therefore, $m\angle CAB = 60°$.

Thus,
$$m\angle ACB + m\angle CAB + m\angle B = 180°$$
$$80° + 60° + m\angle B = 180°$$
$$m\angle B = 40°$$

If you choice was
(B), you found the measure of $\angle$ CED.
(C), you added the two given angles and subtracted the sum from 180°.
(D) you wrote the equation as
$$m\angle ACD + m\angle CAD + m\angle B = 180.$$

6. (B) CAD is a right triangle so use the Pythagorean theorem to find AC.
$$(AC)^2 = (AD)^2 + (CD)^2$$
$$(AC)^2 = 3^2 + 4^2$$
$$(AC)^2 = 9 + 16$$
$$(AC)^2 = 25$$
$$AC = 5$$

If your choice was
(A), you subtracted the lengths of the two legs.
(C), you used $\overline{CD}$ as the hypotenuse and $\overline{AC}$ as a leg.
(D), you found $(AC)^2$ but not AC.

7. (C) The diagonal of the square divides the square into two 45-45-90 triangles. The length of the diagonal is equal to the product of the measure of one of the equal legs and $\sqrt{2}$.

Therefore,
$$d = (3\sqrt{2})\sqrt{2}$$
$$d = 3 \cdot 2$$
$$d = 6$$

If your choice was
- (A), you considered $3\sqrt{2}$ as the hypotenuse and found the length of a leg.
- (B), you found the length of each side of the square.
- (D), you multiplied both 3 and $\sqrt{2}$ by $\sqrt{2}$.

8. (C) The sum of the measures of two sides of a triangle is greater than the measure of the third side. Test each number triplet to see if the sum of any two numbers is greater than the third.

(A)	{3, 5, 9}	$3 + 5 < 9$	No
(B)	{11, 8, 3}	$11 = 8 + 3$	No
(C)	{5, 6, 7}	$5 + 6 > 7$; $6 + 7 > 5$; $5 + 7 > 6$	Yes
(D)	{7, 1, 8}	$7 + 1 = 8$	No

9. (D) Vertical angles are congruent, so $m\angle PRQ = b°$. Therefore, since x is an exterior angle of $\triangle PQR$, $x = a + b$.

If your choice was
- (A), you considered x and a as complementary angles.
- (B), you thought PQR was a right triangle and the nonadjacent anges were 90 and a.
- (C), you found the supplement of x.

10. (D) If $x \neq 90$, then x may be greater or less than 90.
   If $x < 90$, then $(AB)^2 + (BC)^2 > (AC)^2$ and statement A is true.
   If $x > 90$, then $(AB)^2 + (BC)^2 < (AC)^2$ and statement C is true.
   If $(AB)^2 + (BC)^2 = (AC)^2$, then $x = 90$ and statement B cannot be true.

   Thus, it cannot be determined from the information given.

11. (C) In $\triangle ABC$,
$$a + b + 30 = 180$$
$$a + b = 150$$

   In $\triangle DEC$,
$$d + e + 30 = 180$$
$$d + e = 150$$

   Thus, $a + b + d + e = 150 + 150$ or 300.

If your choice was
(A, B, or D), see the solution above.

12. (D) Since the altitude is the leg opposite the 60° angle in the right triangle formed, its measure is one half the product of the measure of the hypotenuse and $\sqrt{3}$.

   Therefore, $a = \frac{1}{2}(6)\sqrt{3} = 3\sqrt{3}$.

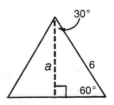

If your choice was
- (A), you found one third the product of the measure of the hypotenuse and $\sqrt{3}$.
- (B), you found the length of the side opposite the 30° angle.
- (C), you used the relationship for the 45-45-90 triangle.

13. **(C)** The two acute angles in a right isosceles triangle each have measures of 45°. Therefore, m∠A = m∠ACB = 45°.

Vertical angles are congruent, so m∠ACB = m∠DCE = 45°.
In △CDE, $d + e + m\angle DCE = 180$
$$d + e + 45 = 180$$
$$d + e = 135$$

> *If your choice was*
> (A), you thought that d and e were acute angles of a right triangle.
> (B), you thought CED was an equilateral triangle.
> (D), you added incorrectly.

14. **(A)** Each angle in △WYZ measures 60°. Therefore, m∠WZX = 120° and m∠ZWX = 30°.

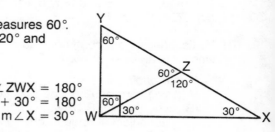

In △WZX;
$$m\angle WZX + m\angle X + m\angle ZWX = 180°$$
$$120° + m\angle X + 30° = 180°$$
$$m\angle X = 30°$$

Thus, WZX is an isosceles triangle and WZ = ZX, so $\frac{WZ}{ZX} = \frac{1}{1}$.

> *If your choice was*
> (B, C, or D), see the solution above.

15. **(D)** Draw a diagram to picture the problem.

Use the Pythagorean theorem to find x and y.

Case 1	*Case 2*
	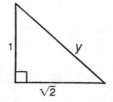

$$x^2 + 1^2 = (\sqrt{2})^2 \qquad\qquad 1^2 + (\sqrt{2})^2 = y^2$$
$$x^2 + 1 = 2 \qquad\qquad\qquad 1 + 2 = y^2$$
$$x^2 = 1 \qquad\qquad\qquad\quad 3 = y^2$$
$$x = 1 \qquad\qquad\qquad\quad \sqrt{3} = y$$

> *If your choice was*
> (A, B, or C), see the solution above.

CIRCLES

1. (B) The measure of inscribed angle ABC is one half the measure of its intercepted arc.

$$m \angle ABC = \tfrac{1}{2} m \widehat{AC}$$
$$m \angle ABC = \tfrac{1}{2} (80°)$$
$$m \angle ABC = 40°$$

If your choice was
(A), you thought the measure of an inscribed angle was $\tfrac{1}{4}$ the measure of its intercepted arc.
(C), you found the measure of the central angle.
(D), you multiplied by 2 instead of $\tfrac{1}{2}$.

2. (C) The measure of inscribed $\angle ABC$ is
$$m \angle ABC = \tfrac{1}{2} m \widehat{AC}$$

The measure of central angle AOC is equal to the measure of its intercepted arc.
$$m \angle AOC = m \widehat{AC}$$

Therefore, $\dfrac{m \angle ABC}{m \angle AOC} = \dfrac{\tfrac{1}{2} m \widehat{AC}}{m \widehat{AC}} = \dfrac{\tfrac{1}{2}}{1} = \tfrac{1}{2}$

If your choice was
(A), you thought that if two angles intercept the same arc, then their measures are equal.
(B), see the solution above.
(D), you found $m \angle AOC : m \angle ABC$.

3. (D) Since the measure of each angle of an equilateral triangle is 60°, $m \angle C = 60°$. Arc AB is intercepted by inscribed $\angle C$.
Therefore, $$m \angle C = \tfrac{1}{2} m \widehat{AB}$$
$$60° = \tfrac{1}{2} m \widehat{AB}$$
$$120° = m \widehat{AB}$$

If your choice was
(A), you solved $60° = \tfrac{1}{2} m \widehat{AB}$ by finding $\tfrac{1}{2}$ of 60°.
(B), you thought the measure of the arc was the same as the measure of its inscribed angle.
(C), you thought that the measure of each angle of an equilateral triangle was 50°.

4. (B) Since the measures of the arcs are in the ratio 2 : 3 : 4,
Let $2x$ = the degree measure of $\widehat{PQ}$
$3x$ = the degree measure of $\widehat{QR}$
$4x$ = the degree measure of $\widehat{RP}$

The degree measure of a circle is 360.
$$2x + 3x + 4x = 360$$
$$9x = 360$$
$$x = 40$$
$$m\overset{\frown}{PQ} = 2x = 80; \; m\overset{\frown}{QR} = 3x = 120; \; m\overset{\frown}{RP} = 4x = 160$$

$\angle\,PQR$ is an inscribed angle and intercepts $\overset{\frown}{RP}$.
$$m\angle PQR = \tfrac{1}{2}m\overset{\frown}{RP}$$
$$m\angle PQR = \tfrac{1}{2}(160)$$
$$m\angle PQR = 80$$

If your choice was
(A), you found only the value of x.
(C), you found $m\overset{\frown}{QR}$.
(D), you found $m\overset{\frown}{RP}$.

5. (B) The intercepted arcs for $\angle\,DEB$ are $\overset{\frown}{BD}$ and $\overset{\frown}{AC}$.
Therefore, $\quad m\angle DEB = \tfrac{1}{2}(m\overset{\frown}{BD} + m\overset{\frown}{AC})$
$$100° = \tfrac{1}{2}(m\overset{\frown}{BD} + 40°)$$
$$200° = m\overset{\frown}{BD} + 40°$$
$$160° = m\overset{\frown}{BD}$$

If your choice was
(A), you thought $\angle\,DEB$ was a central angle.
(C), you thought $\angle\,DEB$ was an inscribed angle.
(D), you thought the measure of $\angle\,DEB$ was one half the difference of the measures of its intercepted arcs and solved the equation incorrectly.

6. (A) $\overline{AB}$ is a diameter and $m\overset{\frown}{AB} = 180°$. Therefore, ACB is a right triangle.
Thus, $\quad$
$$(AB)^2 = (AC)^2 + (CB)^2$$
$$(AB)^2 = 3^2 + 4^2$$
$$(AB)^2 = 9 + 16$$
$$(AB)^2 = 25$$
$$AB = 5$$

The length of radius OA is $\tfrac{1}{2}(5)$ or $2\tfrac{1}{2}$.

If your choice was
(B), you found the length of a diameter.
(C), you thought that the diameter was the sum of the lengths of the chords, 3 and 4.
(D), see (C) above and then you found the length of a radius.

7. (B) The measure of an angle formed by two tangents is one half the difference of the measures of its intercepted arcs:
$$m\angle P = \tfrac{1}{2}\,(m\overset{\frown}{ACB} - m\overset{\frown}{AB})$$

Since the degree measure of a circle is 360,

$$m\overgroup{ACB} + m\overgroup{AB} = 360$$
$$m\overgroup{ACB} + 120 = 360$$
$$m\overgroup{ACB} = 240$$

Therefore, $m\angle P = \frac{1}{2}(240 - 120)°$

$$m\angle P = \frac{1}{2}(120)° = 60°$$

If your choice was
(A), you thought $m\overgroup{ACB} = 180°$.
(C), you thought $m\angle P = \frac{1}{2}m\overgroup{ACB}$.
(D), you thought $m\angle P = \frac{1}{2}(m\overgroup{ACB} + m\overgroup{AB})$.

8. (C) $m\angle DBC = \frac{1}{2}m\overgroup{DC}$ and $m\angle CAD = \frac{1}{2}m\overgroup{DC}$

Thus, $m\angle DBC = m\angle CAD$ and $\angle DBC \cong \angle CAD$.

If your choice was
(A, B, or D), see the solution above.

9. (C) In $\triangle OCB$, $\overline{OC} \cong \overline{OB}$ and $m\angle OCB = m\angle OBC = 25°$.

AOC is an exterior angle of $\triangle OBC$, so
$$m\angle AOC = m\angle OCB + m\angle OBC$$
$$m\angle AOC = 25° + 25° = 50°$$

Since $\overline{AD}$ is a tangent, $m\angle OAD = 90°$.

Thus, $\qquad m\angle ADO + m\angle AOC = 90°$
$$m\angle ADO + 50° = 90°$$
$$m\angle ADO = 40°$$

If your choice was
(A), you thought $m\angle ADO = \frac{1}{2}m\overgroup{AC}$, and $m\overgroup{AC} = 25°$.
(B), you thought $m\angle ADO = \frac{1}{2}m\overgroup{AC}$.
(D), you thought ADO was an isosceles triangle with $\angle ADO \cong \angle AOD$.

10. (C) Since $\overline{BC}$ is a tangent, $m\angle OBC = 90°$ and $\triangle OCB$ is a 30-60-90 triangle. Since OB, the side opposite the 30° angle, is equal to 1, the hypotenuse OC = 2.
$$AC = OC - OA$$
$$AC = 2 - 1$$
$$AC = 1$$

If your choice was
(A), you found the length of $\overline{BC}$.
(B), you found the length of $\overline{OC}$.
(D), you subtracted the length of $\overline{BC}$ from the length of $\overline{OC}$.

11. (A) O is the central angle both for the circle with $\overline{OA}$ as the radius and $\overline{OC}$ as the radius. The measure of the intercepted arcs AB and CD always equals 45°. The length of the radius has no bearing on the size of the arc.

Thus, $m\overset{\frown}{CD} - m\overset{\frown}{AB} = 45° - 45° = 0°$.

> *If your choice was*
> (B, C, or D), see the solution above.

12. (B) $m\angle XYZ = \frac{1}{2}m\overset{\frown}{XWZ}$.

Since XWZ is a semicircle,
$$m\angle XYZ = \frac{1}{2}(180°)$$
$$m\angle XYZ = 90°$$

$\overline{PX}$ is a tangent. Therefore, $m\angle OXP = 90°$.
Thus, $m\angle XYZ = m\angle OXP$.

> *If your choice was*
> (A), you thought $\overset{\frown}{XWZ} = 90°$.
> (C), see the solution above.
> (D), you did not find one half of the intercepted arc.

13. (D) The measure of inscribed $\angle XYZ = \frac{1}{2}m\overset{\frown}{XY}$. The measure of the angle formed by tangent $\overline{PQ}$ and chord $\overline{XY}$ is half the degree measure of the intercepted arc.

Therefore, $m\angle QXY = \frac{1}{2}m\overset{\frown}{XY}$.
Thus, $m\angle QXY = m\angle XZY$, and $\angle QXY \cong \angle XZY$.

> *If your choice was*
> (A), you thought $m\overset{\frown}{WYX} - m\overset{\frown}{WX} = m\overset{\frown}{XY}$.
> (B), you thought $m\overset{\frown}{XY} = m\overset{\frown}{YZ}$.
> (C), you thought XYZ was an isosceles triangle with $\angle XYZ \cong \angle XZY$.

14. (D) ABCD is a quadrilateral inscribed in a circle, so the opposite angles are supplementary.

Thus, $\qquad m\angle ADC + m\angle ABC = 180°$

> *If your choice was*
> (A, B, or C), see the solution above.

15. (C) ADC is an inscribed angle intercepting $\overset{\frown}{ABC}$.
$$m\overset{\frown}{ABC} = m\overset{\frown}{AB} + m\overset{\frown}{BC}$$

BAQ is an angle formed by a tangent and a chord.

Therefore, $\qquad m\angle BAQ = \frac{1}{2}m\overset{\frown}{AB}$

$$60° = \frac{1}{2}m\overset{\frown}{AB}$$
$$120° = m\overset{\frown}{AB}$$

Therefore, $\qquad m\overset{\frown}{ABC} = 120° + 30°$
$$m\overset{\frown}{ABC} = 150°$$

So, $\quad\quad\quad\quad m \angle ADC = \frac{1}{2} m \widehat{ABC}$

$$m \angle ADC = \frac{1}{2}(150°)$$
$$m \angle ADC = 75°$$

If your choice was
(A), you thought $m \angle ADC = \frac{1}{2} m \widehat{BC}$.

(B), you thought $m \angle ADC = \frac{1}{2} m \widehat{AB}$.

(D), you thought that $m \widehat{ABC} = 180°$.

PERIMETER

1. (B) Let P = perimeter

If $\frac{3}{8}$ of the perimeter is 6,

then $\quad\quad\quad\quad\quad \frac{3}{8}P = 6$

and $\quad\quad\quad\quad \frac{8}{3}\left(\frac{3}{8}P\right) = \frac{8}{3}(6)$
$$P = 16$$

Since the length of each side of the equilateral triangle is the same, $\frac{1}{3}$ of $16 = 5\frac{1}{3}$.

If your choice was
(A), you found $\frac{3}{8}$ of 6.

(C), you divided the perimeter by 4.
(D), you found the perimeter but did not find the length of a side.

2. (C) The perimeter P is three times the length of any one side.
$$P = 3(x + 3)$$
$$24 = 3x + 9$$
$$15 = 3x$$
$$5 = x$$
$$8 = x + 3$$

If your choice was
(A), you only found x.
(B), you multiplied $3(x + 3)$ as $3x + 3$ and then found x.
(D), see (B) above and then you found the length of a side.

3. (D) If r is the radius of a circle, the circumference C is given by the formula $C = 2\pi r$.
If the radius r is tripled, the new formula is $C' = 2\pi(3r)$ or $6\pi r$.
Since $6\pi r$ is triple $2\pi r$, the circumference is tripled.

If your choice was
(A), see the solution above.
(B), you thought that tripling the radius meant to raise it to the third power.
(C), you thought that tripling the radius meant to increase it by 3.

4. **(A)** First use the Pythagorean theorem to find EB.

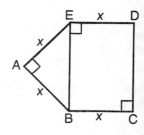

$$(EB)^2 = x^2 + x^2$$
$$(EB)^2 = 2x^2$$
$$EB = \sqrt{2x^2} = x\sqrt{2}$$

Therefore, $EB = DC = x\sqrt{2}$.

Thus, $P = x + x + x\sqrt{2} + x + x$

$$8 + 2\sqrt{2} = 4x + x\sqrt{2}$$
$$2(4 + \sqrt{2}) = x(4 + \sqrt{2})$$
$$2 = x$$

If your choice was
(B), you combined all the lengths of the sides and got $5x\sqrt{2}$.
(C), you added in the length of BE.
(D), you forgot to include the length of DC.

5. **(C)** The side s of the square is the leg of a 45-45-90 triangle, so

$$s = \tfrac{1}{2}(5\sqrt{2})\sqrt{2}$$
$$s = \tfrac{1}{2}(5 \cdot 2)$$
$$s = 5$$

Thus, the perimeter of the square is 4(5) or 20.

If your choice was
(A), you only found a side of the square.
(B), you added the lengths of both diagonals.
(D), you found the area of the square.

6. **(B)** The length of one side of $\triangle ABC$ is 6. Since F is the midpoint of $\overline{AC}$, then $AF = 3$. Since all four sides of a rhombus are equal in length, the perimeter is 4(3) or 12.

If your choice was
(A), you only found the length of a side of the triangle.
(C), you thought the perimeter of the rhombus was equal to the perimeter of the triangle.
(D), you forgot to find half of the length of side AC.

7. **(B)** If the measure of $\overline{AC}$, a leg in right triangle ABC, is half the hypotenuse, $\overline{BC}$, then the measure of the angle opposite $\overline{AC}$ is 30°. $AB = 3\sqrt{3}$ since the measure of the leg opposite the 60° angle is one half the product of the measure of the hypotenuse and $\sqrt{3}$.

The perimeter of $\triangle ABC = 3 + 6 + 3\sqrt{3}$
$$= 9 + 3\sqrt{3}$$

If your choice was
(A), you thought ABC was an isosceles triangle.
(C), you used the properties of the 45-45-90 triangle.
(D), you incorrectly combined $9 + 3\sqrt{3}$ as $12\sqrt{3}$.

8. (C) The diagonals in a rhombus bisect each other and are perpendicular to each other. Therefore, AE = EC = 12 and BE = ED = 9.

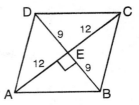

In right triangle AEB,
$$(AB)^2 = 9^2 + 12^2$$
$$(AB)^2 = 81 + 144$$
$$(AB)^2 = 225$$
$$AB = 15$$

The perimeter of the rhombus is 4(15) or 60.

If your choice was
(A), you only found a side of the rhombus.
(B), you found the sum of the lengths of the diagonals.
(D), you found the area of the rhombus.

9. (B) First, form the following ratio : $\dfrac{WZ + ZY + YX}{\text{Perimeter of the rectangle}}$.

$$\frac{a + 3a + a}{a + 3a + a + 3a} = \frac{5a}{8a}$$
$$= \frac{5}{8} = 62\tfrac{1}{2}\%$$

If your choice was
(A), you found the ratio $\dfrac{WZ + ZY}{\text{Perimeter}}$.
(C), you found the sum $a + 3a + a$ as $6a$.
(D), you found the ratio $\dfrac{WZ + ZY + WX}{\text{Perimeter}}$.

10. (D) The two shortest sides, whose lengths are 6 and 15, will be the corresponding sides of the similar triangles.

Thus,
$$\frac{15}{6} = \frac{x}{8} \qquad\qquad \frac{15}{6} = \frac{y}{12}$$
$$6x = 120 \qquad\qquad 6y = 180$$
$$x = 20 \qquad\qquad y = 30$$

Thus, the sides of the larger triangle are 15, 20, and 30. The perimeter is 15 + 20 + 30 = 65.

If your choice was
(A), you found the side of the larger triangle corresponding to the side of the smaller triangle whose length is 8.
(B), you found the side of the larger triangle corresponding to the side of the smaller triangle whose length is 12.
(C), you used 8 and 15 as corresponding sides.

11. (A) If DE = 10, then EF = 10 and FD = 10. Points G, J, and H are the midpoints of the sides of the triangle, so DH = HE = EJ = JF = FG = GD = 5. Since the measure of each angle of △DEF is 60°, the three triangles GDH, JEH, and GFJ are congruent by SAS, and $\overline{GH} \cong \overline{HJ} \cong \overline{GJ}$. Therefore, △GJH is equilateral and the length of each side is 5.

Thus, the perimeter of △GJH is 15.

If your choice was
(B, C, or D), see the solution above.

12. **(C)** Let w = the measure of the width
               $5w - 2$ = the measure of the length

Then, $w + 5w - 2 + w + 5w - 2 = 32$
                             $12w - 4 = 32$
                             $12w = 36$
                             $w = 3$
                   $5w - 2 = 5(3) - 2 = 13$

If your choice was
(A), you only found the measure of the width.
(B), you wrote $2w - 5$ instead of $5w - 2$.
(D), you wrote the equation, $w + 5w - 2 = 32$.

13. **(B)** Tangents $\overline{PA}$ and $\overline{PB}$ are equal in length, so PA = PB = 12 and OA = OB = 5.
The perimeter of BPAO is $12 + 12 + 5 + 5 = 34$.

If your choice was
(A), you found only the sum $5 + 12$.
(C), you found OP = 13, and the perimeter of $\triangle$OAP.
(D), see the solution above.

14. **(C)** EB = AB − AE, so EB = 7 − 3 = 4.
Since tangent segments drawn to a circle from the same exterior point are congruent, AE = AD = 3, EB = BF = 4, and FC = DC = 2.
Thus, $P = AB + BC + CA$
                        $P = 7 + (4 + 2) + (2 + 3)$
                        $P = 7 + 6 + 5$
                        $P = 18$

If your choice was
(A), you found the sum of the segments AE + BF + DC.
(B), you found the sum of the three given lengths.
(D), you found twice the sum of the given lengths.

15. **(D)** If r is the radius of a circle, the circumference C is given by the formula $C = 2\pi r$.
So, $1 = 2\pi r$
                   $\frac{1}{2\pi} = r$

If your choice was
(A), you found the diameter of the circle.
(B), you forgot to include π in your answer.
(C), you divided the right side of the equation by 2π and subtracted 2π from the left side.

AREA

1. **(B)** If r is the radius of a circle, the area A is given by the formula $A = \pi r^2$.
So, $A = \pi(4)^2$
                   $A = \pi \cdot 16$
                   $A = 16\pi$

If your choice was
(A), you found 4^2 as 8 instead of 16.
(C), you forgot to include π in the formula.
(D), you used the length of the diameter for the radius in the formula.

2. (A) The area A of a rhombus is equal to one half the product of the length of its diagonals d_1 and d_2.
$$A = \tfrac{1}{2} d_1 d_2$$
$$A = \tfrac{1}{2} (6)(9)$$
$$A = 27$$

If your choice was
(B), your multiplication is faulty: $6 \times 9 = 54$.
(C), you found the product of $\tfrac{1}{2}$ of 6 and $\tfrac{1}{2}$ of 9.
(D), you forgot to find half of the product.

3. (B) Use the formula for the area of a trapezoid.
$$A = \tfrac{1}{2}h(b_1 + b_2)$$
$$A = \tfrac{1}{2}(4)(7 + 12)$$
$$A = 2(19)$$
$$A = 38$$

If your choice was
(A), you found the sum of the three given lengths.
(C), you forgot to find half of the product.
(D), you found the product of the three given lengths.

4. (B) Use the formula for the area of a triangle.
$$A = \tfrac{1}{2}bh$$
$$48 = \tfrac{1}{2}(16)h$$
$$48 = 8h$$
$$6 = h$$

If your choice was
(A), you multiplied both 48 and 16 by $\tfrac{1}{2}$.
(C), your division is faulty: $48 \div 8 \neq 7$.
(D), you multiplied the left side of the equation by 2 and the right side by $\tfrac{1}{2}$.

5. (A) If r is the radius of a circle, the area A is given by the formula $A = \pi r^2$.

If the radius r is tripled, then the new formula becomes
$$A' = \pi (3r)^2$$
$$A' = 9\pi r^2$$
Since $9\pi r^2$ is 9 times πr^2, the new area is multiplied by 9.

If your choice was
(B), you thought that tripling the radius resulted in raising it to the third power.
(C), you thought that tripling the radius meant to increase it by 3.
(D), you forgot to square 3 which resulted in $3\pi r^2$.

6. (D) The central angle, $120°$, is $\frac{1}{3}$ of $360°$, so the length of the arc is $\frac{1}{3}$ the circumference of the circle.
$$8\pi = \frac{1}{3}(2\pi r)$$
$$24\pi = 2\pi r$$
$$12 = r$$
The area of a circle is given by the formula $A = \pi r^2$.
$$A = \pi(12)^2$$
$$A = 144\pi$$

If your choice was
(A), you forgot to find $\frac{1}{3}$ of the circumference.
(B), you found 12^2 as 24 instead of 144.
(C), you forgot to include π in your answer.

7. (C) The formula for the area of a square is $A = s^2$.
$$A = 4^2 \text{ or } 16$$
The two semicircles together form one complete circle of radius 2. The area of a circle is given by the formula $A = \pi r^2$.
$$A = \pi(2)^2$$
$$A = 4\pi$$
The area of the shaded portion is the area of the square less the area of the two semicircles:
$$A = 16 - 4\pi$$

If your choice was
(A), you found 4^2 as 2×4 or 8.
(B), see (A) above, and you forgot to find the square of the radius.
(D), you forgot to find the square of the radius.

8. (A) The length of the hypotenuse or side s is twice the length of the side opposite the $60°$ angle divided by $\sqrt{3}$.
Therefore, $s = \frac{2(3\sqrt{3})}{\sqrt{3}}$

$$s = 6$$

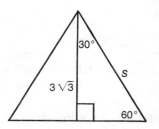

Use the formula $A = \frac{s^2\sqrt{3}}{4}$

$$A = \frac{6^2}{4}\sqrt{3}$$
$$A = \frac{36}{4}\sqrt{3} = 9\sqrt{3}$$

If your choice was
(B), you forgot to include the $\sqrt{3}$.
(C), you found the side of the triangle as $6\sqrt{3}$.
(D), you only found the length of a side.

120

9. (B) From points D and C, $\overline{DE}$ and $\overline{CF}$ are drawn perpendicular to base $\overline{AB}$. Rectangle DEFC is formed and DC = EF = 8.

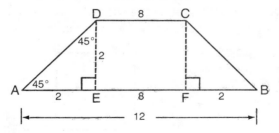

Since ABCD is an isosceles trapezoid, $\triangle AED \cong \triangle BFC$ and AE = BF = 2. AED is an isosceles triangle with AE = DE. Therefore, DE = 2.

The area of a trapezoid is given by the formula
$$A = \tfrac{1}{2}h(b_1 + b_2)$$
$$A = \tfrac{1}{2}(2)(8 + 12)$$
$$A = 20$$

If your choice was
(A), you found the length of the altitude as $\sqrt{2}$.
(C), you forgot to include one half in the formula.
(D), you found the length of the altitude as 8.

10. (C) The total surface area of a rectangular prism is given by the formula $S = 2(\ell h + \ell w + wh)$.
Substitute, $\ell = 4$, $w = 4$, and $h = 3$.
Therefore,
$$S = 2(4 \cdot 3 + 4 \cdot 4 + 4 \cdot 3)$$
$$S = 2(12 + 16 + 12)$$
$$S = 2(40) = 80 \text{ cm}^2$$

If your choice was
(A), you found the volume of the prism.
(B), you found only the lateral area.
(D), you thought four faces measured 4 by 4.

11. (D) Let each equal segment have length x. Then, the area of the square is $(3x)^2$ or $9x^2$.
The area of each right triangle is given by the formula $A = \tfrac{1}{2}\ell_1\ell_2$.
The two right triangles have legs of lengths x and $2x$.
$$A = \tfrac{1}{2}(x)(2x) = x^2$$
The third triangle has legs of lengths $2x$ and $2x$.
$$A = \tfrac{1}{2}(2x)(2x) = 2x^2$$
The area of the shaded portion is the area of the square minus the area of the three triangles.
$$A = 9x^2 - (x^2 + x^2 + 2x^2)$$
$$A = 9x^2 - 4x^2 \text{ or } 5x^2$$

Thus, $\dfrac{\text{Area of shaded region}}{\text{Area of square}} = \dfrac{5x^2}{9x^2} = \dfrac{5}{9}$.

If your choice was

(A), you found $\dfrac{\text{Area of unshaded region}}{\text{Area of square}}$.

(B), you found the area of the shaded region as $4\frac{1}{2}x^2$.

(C), you forgot to use one half in the area formula.

12. (D) Since the perimeter of square X is triple that of square Y, $P_x = 3P_y$.

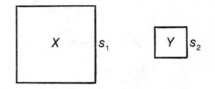

The perimeter of X, if each side has length s_1, is $4s_1$.
The perimeter of Y, if each side has length s_2, is $4s_2$.

Therefore,
$$4s_1 = 3(4s_2)$$
$$4s_1 = 12s_2$$
$$s_1 = 3s_2$$

The area of X is $(s_1)^2$ or $(9s_2)^2$. The area of Y is $(s_2)^2$ so the area of X is 9 times the area of Y.

If your choice was

(A), you found how the area of Y is related to the area of X.

(B), you forgot to square 3 in $(3s_2)^2$.

(C), you squared 3 as $2 \cdot 3 = 6$.

13. (B) The area of a circle is given by the formula $A = \pi r^2$.
$$\frac{9}{\pi} = \pi r^2$$
$$\frac{9}{\pi^2} = r^2$$
$$\frac{3}{\pi} = r \text{ and } d = 2\left(\frac{3}{\pi}\right) = \frac{6}{\pi}$$

When unfolded, the circumference of the base is the same length as the length of the rectangle.
Therefore,
$$C = \pi d$$
$$C = \pi\left(\frac{6}{\pi}\right)$$
$$C = 6$$
Thus, the length of the rectangle is 6 cm.

If your choice was

(A), you used the area of the base as 9π.

(C), you found only the diameter of the circle.

(D), see the solution above.

14. (D) If two lines are parallel, then the perpendicular distance between them is always the same.

Area of $\triangle PQR = \frac{1}{2}(PR)(h_1)$

Area of $\triangle PSR = \frac{1}{2}(PR)(h_2)$

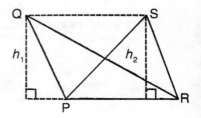

Since the heights are the same length for both triangles, $h_1 = h_2$, the areas are equal.

If your choice was
(A, B, or C), see the solution above.

15. (D) The area is not uniquely determined. The area of $\triangle ABC$ is given by the formula
$$A = \tfrac{1}{2}(AC)(BC)$$
$$9 = \tfrac{1}{2}(AC)(BC)$$
$$18 = (AC)(BC)$$
Therefore, the product of the two legs is 18.

Use the Pythagorean theorem to find the length of diameter AB. If $AC = 2$ and $BC = 9$, then $AB = \sqrt{85}$ and if $AC = 3$ and $BC = 6$, then $AB = \sqrt{45}$.

If your choice was
(A, B, or C), see the solution above.

VOLUME

1. (B) The volume of a rectangular prism is given by the formula $V = \ell wh$.
$$V = 5(2)(3)$$
$$V = 30$$

If your choice was
(A), you found the sum of the three dimensions.
(C), you found the surface area of the figure.
(D), you multiplied both 2 and 3 by 5.

2. (C) A cube has six square faces whose edges are all congruent. Therefore, the area of each face is $6x^2 \div 6 = x^2$, and the length of each edge is x.
Since the volume of a cube is e^3, the volume is x^3.

If your choice was
(A), you found the area of each face.
(B), you found the sum of the areas of 4 faces.
(D), you found the volume of 6 such cubes.

3. (C) If the edge of each cube is e, then the volume is e^3. The volume is 125 so,
$$V = e^3$$
$$125 = e^3$$
$$5 = e$$
A cube has 12 edges, so the sum of the lengths of the edges is $12(5) = 60$.

If your choice was
(A), you found the length of an edge.
(B), you thought a cube had 8 edges.
(D), you found the surface area of the cube.

4. (D) Since the height h is one half the diameter d, then $h = \frac{1}{2}d$. If r is the radius, then $d = 2r$ and $h = r$.
The volume of a right circular cylinder is given by the formula $V = \pi r^2 h$.

Since $h = r$, the formula becomes $V = \pi r^2(r)$ and $V = \pi r^3$. If $r = 4$, $V = \pi(4)^3$ or 64π.

If your choice was
(A), you found only the area of the base.
(B), you multiplied $4 \times 4 \times 4$ as 8×4.
(C), see the solution above.

5. (D) The volume V of a sphere of radius r is given by the formula
$$V = \frac{4}{3}\pi r^3$$
$$V = \frac{4}{3}\pi(6)^3$$
$$V = \frac{4}{3}\pi(216)$$
$$V = 288\pi$$

If your choice was
(A), you found the length of a diameter.
(B), you found the surface area.
(C), you forgot to multiply πr^3 by $\frac{4}{3}$.

6. (C) The volume V of a right circular cone of radius r and height h is given by the formula $V = \frac{1}{3}\pi r^2 h$.
If the radius is doubled, the new volume V' is
$$V' = \frac{1}{3}\pi(2r)^2 h$$
$$V' = \frac{1}{3}\pi(4r^2)h$$
$$V' = \frac{4}{3}\pi r^2 h$$
The new volume, $4\left(\frac{1}{3}\pi r^2 h\right)$, is four times as large.

If your choice was
(A), you thought that doubling the radius had no effect on the volume.
(B), you forgot to square 2 in $(2r)^2$.
(D), you cubed 2 instead of squaring it.

7. (D) Testing each of the given choices results in choice D as the only one that will form a closed rectangular prism with no overlaps.

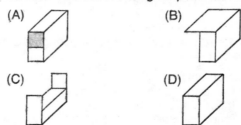

8. **(A)** The volume of a right circular cylinder is given by the formula $V = \pi r^2 h$.

Test each of the given choices.
(A) If $r = 2$ and $h = 9$, then $V = \pi(4)(9) = 36\pi$.
(B) If $r = 3$ and $h = 8$, then $V = \pi(9)(8) = 72\pi$.
(C) If $r = 6$ and $h = 2$, then $V = \pi(36)(2) = 72\pi$.
(D) If $r = 4$ and $h = 4.5$, then $V = \pi(16)(4.5) = 72\pi$.

Thus, choice (A) does not have the same volume.

9. **(A)** If the edge of each cube has length $\frac{1}{2}$, then the dimensions of 5 by 2 by 4 are $2\frac{1}{2}$ by 1 by 2. The volume of the rectangular solid is given by the formula $V = \ell wh$.

$$V = 2\tfrac{1}{2} \times 1 \times 2$$
$$V = 5$$

If your choice was
(B), you found the volume of the rectangular solid with each cube of length 1.
(C), you found the volume of the rectangular solid with each cube of length 2.
(D), you found the volume of one cube.

10. **(B)** The volume V of a cube with edge e is given by the formula $V = e^3$.

If $e = \sqrt{3}$, $V = (\sqrt{3})^3$
               $V = \sqrt{3} \cdot \sqrt{3} \cdot \sqrt{3} = 3\sqrt{3}$
If $e = \sqrt[3]{3}$, $V = (\sqrt[3]{3})^3$
               $V = \sqrt[3]{3} \cdot \sqrt[3]{3} \cdot \sqrt[3]{3} = 3$

Thus, $\dfrac{3\sqrt{3}}{3} = \dfrac{\overset{1}{\cancel{3}}\sqrt{3}}{\underset{1}{\cancel{3}}} = \sqrt{3}$.

If your choice was
(A), you found $(\sqrt{3})^3$ as $3\sqrt[3]{3}$.
(B), you cancelled the $\sqrt{3}$ and 3 in the fraction $\frac{3\sqrt{3}}{3}$.
(D), you found the volume of the cube with edge $\sqrt{3}$ as $9\sqrt{3}$.

11. **(A)** If X contains $\frac{1}{3}x$ cubic units of fluid and if Y contains $\frac{1}{4}y$ cubic units of fluid, then the total amount of fluid is $\frac{1}{3}x + \frac{1}{4}y$ cubic units. Since the fluid is to be divided equally among the 3 containers, each container gets one third of the total, or $\frac{\frac{1}{3}x + \frac{1}{4}y}{3}$. The part of Z that is filled is the amount of fluid over the volume of Z or

$$\frac{\dfrac{\frac{1}{3}x + \frac{1}{4}y}{3}}{z} \quad \text{or} \quad \frac{\frac{1}{3}x + \frac{1}{4}y}{3z}$$

Simplifying the complex fraction results in

$$\frac{12\left(\frac{1}{3}x + \frac{1}{4}y\right)}{12\,(3z)} = \frac{4x + 3y}{36z}$$

If your choice was
(B), you found the amount of fluid in Z as $\frac{x + y}{3}$.
(C), you forgot to divide $\frac{1}{3}x + \frac{1}{4}y$ by 3.
(D), you combined unlike terms $4x + 3y$.

12. (B) The volumes of A and B are given by the formula $V = \frac{1}{2}\ell wh$.

Volume of A: $V = \frac{4 \cdot 2 \cdot 9}{2} = 36$

Volume of B: $V = \frac{3 \cdot 3 \cdot 8}{2} = 36$

Thus, volume of A = volume of B or A = B.

If your choice was
(A, C, or D), see the solution above.

13. (B) A cube has six faces. If 4 faces of each cube have pictures, then 2 faces of each cube have letters.
In a set of 36 cubic blocks, there are 2×36 or 72 faces with letters.

If your choice was
(A), see the solution above.
(C), you found the number of faces that have numbers.
(D), you found the total number of faces.

14. (D) The diameter of the largest sphere is $h - 1$ since it must fit into the smallest dimension of the cylinder.
Therefore, the radius is $\frac{h - 1}{2}$.

If your choice was
(A), you found the diameter of the sphere.
(B or C), a sphere of diameter h and radius $\frac{h}{2}$ is unable to fit into the diameter of the sphere which is smaller than h.

15. (A) Construct a table to find all possible sums.

Second die

+	1	2	3	4	5	6
1	②	③	④	⑤	⑥	⑦
2	3	4	5	6	7	⑧
3	4	5	6	7	8	⑨
4	5	6	7	8	9	⑩
5	6	7	8	9	10	⑪
6	7	8	9	10	11	⑫

First die

1, 1; 1, 2; 1, 3; 1, 4; 1, 5; and 1, 6 will form 1 set of sums.
Proceed in the same way with 2 on the first die. The only new
sum will be 8. Continuing in this manner will result in new
sums of 9, 10, 11, and 12.
Thus, there will be 11 such sums.

If your choice was
(B), you included 1 in your sums.
(C), see the solution above.
(D), you included all possible sums, not different sums.

COORDINATE GEOMETRY

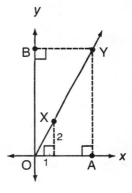

1. (B) Drop a perpendicular from point X to
the x-axis. The slope of $\overline{OX}$ and $\overline{OY}$
is $\frac{2}{1}$ or 2. Since OA = 3, then
$\overline{AY} = 2 \times 3 = 6$ and the coordinates
of Y are (3, 6).
Thus, the coordinates of B are (0, 6).

If your choice was
(A), you reversed the x- and y- coordinates.
(C), see the solution above.
(D), you found the coordinates of point Y.

2. (A) Since A is equidistant from B and C, it
is the midpoint of $\overline{BC}$ if it is on $\overline{BC}$.
Use the midpoint formula

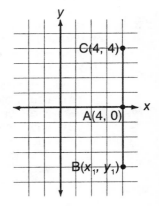

$$\bar{x} = \frac{x_1 + x_2}{2} \qquad \bar{y} = \frac{y_1 + y_2}{2}$$

where $\bar{x} = 4$ and $\bar{y} = 0$. Since C is
(4, 4), let $x_2 = 4$ and $y_2 = 4$ and the
coordinates of B = (x_1, y_1).

$$4 = \frac{x_1 + 4}{2} \qquad 0 = \frac{y_1 + 4}{2}$$
$$8 = x_1 + 4 \qquad 0 = y_1 + 4$$
$$4 = x_1 \qquad -4 = y_1$$

The coordinates of B are $(4, -4)$.

If your choice was
(B, C, or D), see the solution above.

3. (C) The slope-intercept form of the equation of a straight line with
slope m and y-intercept b is $y = mx + b$.
If the slope of the line is $-\frac{2}{3}$, then the equation of the line is of
the form $y = -\frac{2}{3}x + b$.

The line passes through the point (0, 0) so substitute
(0, 0) for x and y in the equation

$$y = -\tfrac{2}{3}x + b$$

$$0 = -\tfrac{2}{3}(0) + b$$

$$0 = b$$

The equation of the line is $y = -\tfrac{2}{3}x$ or $3y + 2x = 0$.

If your choice was
(A, B, or D), see the solution above.

4. (B) If $\overline{AM}$ is a median, M must be the midpoint of $\overline{BC}$. Use the
midpoint formula to find $M(\overline{x}, \overline{y})$ given (x_1, y_1) as (6, 1) and
(x_2, y_2) as (4, 5).

$$\overline{x} = \frac{x_1 + x_2}{2} \qquad\qquad \overline{y} = \frac{y_1 + y_2}{2}$$

$$\overline{x} = \frac{6 + 4}{2} \qquad\qquad \overline{y} = \frac{1 + 5}{2}$$

$$\overline{x} = 5 \qquad\qquad \overline{y} = 3$$

The coordinates of M are (5, 3).

If your choice was
(A), you found the midpoint of $\overline{AB}$.
(C), you forgot to find half of each sum.
(D), you found the midpoint of $\overline{AC}$.

5. (C) The equation of a line parallel to the
x-axis and at a distance a below it
is $y = -a$. Since $a = 4$, the equation
is $y = -4$.

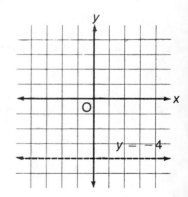

If your choice was
(A), you wrote the equation of the
line 4 units above the x-axis.
(B), you wrote the equation of the
line parallel to the y-axis and 4
units to the left of it.
(D), you wrote the equation of the
line parallel to the y-axis and 4
units to the right of it.

6. (B) The circle with its center at the origin and radius r has the
equation $x^2 + y^2 = r^2$. Use the distance formula to find the
length of the radius $\overline{QP}$.
Let $x_1 = 0$, $y_1 = 0$ and $x_2 = 3$, $y_2 = 4$.

Therefore,
$$r = \sqrt{(x_2 - x_1)^2 + (y_2 - y_1)^2}$$
$$r = \sqrt{(3 - 0)^2 + (4 - 0)^2}$$
$$r = \sqrt{3^2 + 4^2}$$
$$r = \sqrt{9 + 16}$$
$$r = \sqrt{25}$$
$$r = 5$$

Thus, $x^2 + y^2 = 5^2$ or $x^2 + y^2 = 25$.

If your choice was
(A), you forgot to square each of the terms.
(C), you thought the length of the radius was 3.
(D), you thought the length of the radius was 4.

7. (B) The length of the line segment joining two points (x_1, y_1) and (x_2, y_2) is given by the formula

$$d = \sqrt{(x_2 - x_1)^2 + (y_2 - y_1)^2}$$

Let $x_1 = -1$, $y_1 = 1$ and $x_2 = 2$, $y_2 = 3$.

Then,
$$d = \sqrt{[2 - (-1)]^2 + (3 - 1)^2}$$
$$d = \sqrt{(2 + 1)^2 + 2^2}$$
$$d = \sqrt{3^2 + 2^2}$$
$$d = \sqrt{9 + 4}$$
$$d = \sqrt{13}$$

If your choice was
(A), you simplified $2 - (-1)$ as 1 and then forgot to find the square root of 5.
(C), you simplified $2 - (-1)$ as 1.
(D), you forgot to find the square root.

8. (D) The slope m of the line passing through two points (x_1, y_1) and (x_2, y_2) is given by the formula
$$m = \frac{y_2 - y_1}{x_2 - x_1}$$

Let $x_2 = 2$, $y_2 = 7$ and $x_1 = 8$, $y_1 = -1$.

Then,
$$m = \frac{7 - (-1)}{2 - 8}$$
$$m = \frac{7 + 1}{-6} = \frac{8}{-6} \text{ or } -\frac{4}{3}$$

The equation of the line passing through the point (x_1, y_1) and having slope m is
$$y - y_1 = m(x - x_1)$$

Let $x_1 = 2$, $y_1 = 7$ and substitute $-\frac{4}{3}$ for m.

$$y - 7 = -\frac{4}{3}(x - 2)$$

Multiply both sides by 3.
$$3(y - 7) = -4(x - 2)$$
$$3y - 21 = -4x + 8$$
$$4x + 3y = 29$$

If your choice was
(A), you wrote $3(y - 7)$ as $3y - 7$.
(B), you wrote $-4(x - 2)$ as $-4x - 8$.
(C), you wrote $-4(x - 2)$ as $-4x - 2$.

9. (A) The opposite sides of a parallelogram
are parallel and equal in length, so AB = DC.

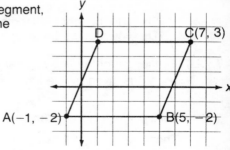

Since $\overline{AB}$ is a horizontal line segment,
its length is the difference of the
x-coordinates.
AB = 5 − (−1) = 6
Therefore, DC = 6 and the
x-coordinate of D is
$$6 = 7 - x$$
$$x = 1$$
Thus the coordinates of D
are (1, 3).

If your choice was
(B), you thought the x-coordinates of D and A were equal.
(C), you thought the x-coordinates of D and B were equal.
(D), you solved 6 = 7 − x incorrectly as x = 13.

10. (C) If the area of the circle is 16π square
units, then

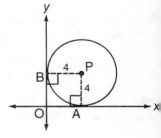

$$A = \pi r^2$$
$$16\pi = \pi r^2$$
$$16 = r^2$$
$$4 = r$$

Since the x- and y-axes are tangent to
circle P, $\overline{PA}$ and $\overline{PB}$ are the radii of
circle P. Thus, the coordinates of
P are (4, 4).

If your choice was
(A or B), you found two factors of 16.
(D), you thought the diameter was
4 units in length.

11. (B) Use the formula $A = \frac{1}{2}bh$.

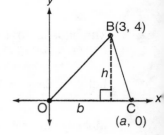

The height of the triangle is the
y-coordinate of B or 4. The base of the
triangle is the x-coordinate of C or a.
Then, $\qquad 10 = \frac{1}{2}(a)(4)$
$$10 = 2a$$
$$5 = a$$

If your choice was
(A), you forgot to multiply by one half.
(C), you used the x-coordinate of B as the height of $\triangle OCB$.
(D), you divided the left side of the equation by 2 and
multiplied the right side by 2.

12. (C) Since $\overline{WX}$ is a horizontal line segment, its length is found by
the difference of the x-coordinates.
$$WX = 5 - (-2)$$
$$WX = 5 + 2 = 7$$
Since WX = YZ, YZ = 7.

$\overline{YZ}$ is a vertical line segment and its length is found by the difference of its y-coordinates.

$$YZ = y_2 - y_1$$
$$7 = 5 - y_1$$
$$y_1 = -2$$

Thus, the coordinates of Z are $(2, -2)$.

If your choice was
(A, B, or D), see the solution above.

13. (A) For two lines to be perpendicular, the slope of one line must be the negative reciprocal of the slope of the other line.

Write the equation of the given line in the slope-intercept form, $y = mx + b$, where m represents the slope.

$$3y + 2x = 12$$
$$3y = -2x + 12$$
$$y = -\tfrac{2}{3}x + 4 \qquad \left(m = -\tfrac{2}{3}\right)$$

The negative reciprocal of $-\tfrac{2}{3}$ is $\tfrac{3}{2}$.

If your choice was
(B. C, or D), see the solution above.

14. (D) ROP is a 30-60-90 triangle. The x-coordinate of R is the same as the length of $\overline{OP}$, 2. The measure of OR = 4.

The y-coordinate of R is the same as the length of $\overline{RP}$. $\overline{RP}$ is the side opposite the 60° angle in $\triangle ORP$ and its measure is $2\sqrt{3}$.

Thus, the coordinates of R are $(2, 2\sqrt{3})$.

If your choice was
(A), you thought $\triangle ORP$ was an isosceles triangle.
(B), you used the 45-45-90 triangle relationship.
(C), you reversed the x- and y-coordinates.

15. (D) For two lines to be parallel, their slopes must be equal. The slope m of a line passing through two points, (x_1, y_1) and (x_2, y_2), is given by the formula

$$m = \frac{y_2 - y_1}{x_2 - x_1}$$

Let $x_1 = 2$, $y_1 = 1$ and $x_2 = 5$, $y_2 = 5$.

$$m = \frac{5 - 1}{5 - 2} = \frac{4}{3}$$

Use the slope-intercept form of the equation of the straight line.

$$y = mx + b$$

Substitute $\tfrac{4}{3}$ for m and since the line passes through the origin, the y-intercept b is 0.

$$y = \tfrac{4}{3}x + 0$$

$$y = \tfrac{4}{3}x \quad \text{or} \quad 3y = 4x$$

PROBLEM SOLVING

1. (C) If two chords are parallel, then they intercept equal arcs on a circle. Therefore, $m\overset{\frown}{HA} = m\overset{\frown}{GF} = 50°$. It is known, that $\overset{\frown}{DG} \cong \overset{\frown}{GF}$, so $m\overset{\frown}{GF} = m\overset{\frown}{DG} = 50°$.

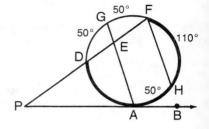

   ∠P is formed by a tangent and a secant, and its intercepted arcs are FHA and DA.

$$m\overset{\frown}{FHA} = m\overset{\frown}{FH} + m\overset{\frown}{HA}$$
$$= 110° + 50°$$
$$m\overset{\frown}{FHA} = 160°$$

   Since the sum of the measures of all the arcs of a circle is 360°, then

$$m\overset{\frown}{HA} + m\overset{\frown}{DA} + m\overset{\frown}{DG} + m\overset{\frown}{GF} + m\overset{\frown}{FH} = 360°$$
$$50° + m\overset{\frown}{DA} + 50° + 50° + 110° = 360°$$
$$260° + m\overset{\frown}{DA} = 360°$$
$$m\overset{\frown}{DA} = 100°$$

$$m\angle P = \tfrac{1}{2}(m\overset{\frown}{FHA} - m\overset{\frown}{DA})$$
$$m\angle P = \tfrac{1}{2}(160° - 100°)$$
$$m\angle P = \tfrac{1}{2}(60°)$$
$$m\angle P = 30°$$

If your choice was

(A), you thought the intercepted arc was $\overset{\frown}{FH}$ instead of $\overset{\frown}{FHA}$.

(B), you left out $m\overset{\frown}{DG}$ when finding $m\overset{\frown}{DA}$ and then subtracted $m\overset{\frown}{FH}$ from $m\overset{\frown}{DA}$.

(D), you found half of the sum of the intercepted arcs.

2. (C) Draw line segments AC and DB to form similar triangles AXC and DXB. Then form the proportion

$$\frac{AX}{XD} = \frac{CX}{XB}$$

   Therefore,
$$(AX)(XB) = (CX)(XD)$$
$$(8)(5) = 10(XD)$$
$$40 = 10(XD)$$
$$4 = XD$$

   Thus,
$$CD = CX + XD$$
$$CD = 10 + 4 = 14$$

If your choice was
(A), you thought that AX + XB = CX + XD.
(B), you found only the length of $\overline{XD}$.
(D), you found XD = 4 and then multiplied CX by XD.

3. (B) Right triangles BFA and EFD are similar to each other since vertical angles BFA and EFD are congruent and alternate interior angles ABF and DEF are also congruent.

Since
$$BC = AF + FD$$
$$10 = AF + 7.5$$
$$2.5 = AF$$

If two triangles are similar, their corresponding sides are in proportion.
$$\frac{AB}{DE} = \frac{AF}{DF}$$
$$\frac{AB}{9} = \frac{2.5}{7.5} = \frac{25}{75}$$
$$\frac{AB}{9} = \frac{1}{3}$$
$$3(AB) = 9$$
$$AB = 3$$

If your choice was
(A), you thought that $\triangle$AFB was isosceles.
(C or D), see the solution above.

4. (D) In a regular polygon of n sides, the measure of one angle is given by the formula
$$\frac{(n-2)180°}{n}$$

In a regular pentagon, $n = 5$: $\frac{(5-2)180°}{5} = \frac{3(180°)}{5} = 108°$

In a regular octagon, $n = 8$: $\frac{(8-2)180°}{8} = \frac{6(180°)}{8} = 135°$

Thus, $\frac{x}{y} = \frac{108°}{135°} = \frac{4}{5}$ or 4 : 5.

If your choice was
(A), you found the ratio of the number of sides in each polygon.
(B), you thought an octagon had 10 sides.
(C), you thought a pentagon had 6 sides.

5. (C) Since $m\angle 1 = m\angle 2 = m\angle 3$, $\triangle$AEB is equiangular. Each angle measures 60°. If $\triangle$DEA $\cong$ $\triangle$AEB, $\triangle$DEA is also equiangular and $m\angle 4 = m\angle 5 = m\angle 6 = 60°$.

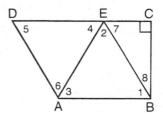

The sum of the measures of angles 4, 2, and 7 is 180°. Therefore, $m\angle 7 = 60°$ and BEC is a 30-60-90 triangle.

If AB = 4, then BE = AE = AD = DE = 4.

So, BC $= \frac{1}{2}(4)\sqrt{3} = 2\sqrt{3}$.

Since AD $= 4$, $\frac{BC}{AD} = \frac{2\sqrt{3}}{4} = \frac{\sqrt{3}}{2}$ or $\sqrt{3} : 2$.

If your choice was
(A), you thought that $\overline{BC} \cong \overline{AD}$.
(B), you found the ratio of EC to AD.
(D), you reversed the terms of the ratio.

6. (C) In $\triangle ADB$,
$$x + z + y + 80 = 180$$
$$x + z + y = 100$$

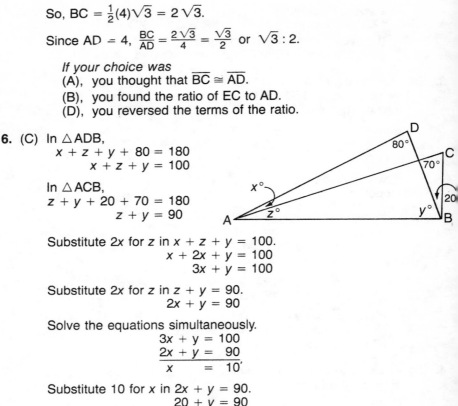

In $\triangle ACB$,
$$z + y + 20 + 70 = 180$$
$$z + y = 90$$

Substitute $2x$ for z in $x + z + y = 100$.
$$x + 2x + y = 100$$
$$3x + y = 100$$

Substitute $2x$ for z in $z + y = 90$.
$$2x + y = 90$$

Solve the equations simultaneously.
$$3x + y = 100$$
$$2x + y = 90$$
$$\overline{x = 10}$$

Substitute 10 for x in $2x + y = 90$.
$$20 + y = 90$$
$$y = 70$$

If your choice was
(A), you found the value of x.
(B), you found the value of z.
(D), you found the sum of y and 20.

7. (C) The area of the square is s^2. The area of the equilateral triangle is $\frac{s^2}{4}\sqrt{3}$. The area of the rectangle is $2s^2$. The fraction of the area of the rectangle that is uncovered is $1 - $ (fraction that is covered).

The covered fractional part is
$$\frac{\text{Area of square} + \text{Area of equilateral triangle}}{\text{Area of rectangle}}$$

$$\frac{s^2 + \frac{s^2}{4}\sqrt{3}}{2s^2} = \frac{4s^2 + s^2\sqrt{3}}{8s^2} = \frac{4 + \sqrt{3}}{8}$$

Thus, the uncovered fractional part is

$$1 - \left(\frac{4 + \sqrt{3}}{8}\right) = \frac{8}{8} - \left(\frac{4 + \sqrt{3}}{8}\right) = \frac{4 - \sqrt{3}}{8}$$

134

If your choice was
(A), you found the fractional part of the rectangle that is covered.
(B), you simplified $\frac{4 + \sqrt{3}}{8}$ as $\frac{4}{8} + \sqrt{3}$.
(D), you simplified $\frac{4 - \sqrt{3}}{8}$ as $\frac{4}{8} - \sqrt{3}$.

8. (A) A wheel rotating at 10 revolutions per minute makes 1 revolution in 6 seconds. In 18 seconds it makes 3 revolutions and travels 15 feet. Thus, the wheel travels 5 feet per revolution. 5 feet must be the circumference of the wheel.

Thus,
$$C = \pi d$$
$$5 = \pi d$$
$$\frac{5}{\pi} = d$$

The diameter of the wheel is $\frac{5}{\pi}$ feet.

If your choice was
(B), you used the distance the wheel traveled in 3 revolutions.
(C), you solved $5 = \pi d$ by multiplying the left side by π and dividing the right side by π.
(D), you found the length of the radius.

9. (D) The area of $\triangle$DEF is $\frac{1}{2}h(\text{DE})$.

The area of trapezoid DECA is $\frac{1}{2}h(\text{DE} + \text{AC})$.

Therefore, $\dfrac{\frac{1}{2}h(\text{DE})}{\frac{1}{2}h(\text{DE} + \text{AC})} = \dfrac{\text{DE}}{\text{DE} + \text{AC}}$

This ratio is not constant because for the same triangle DEF, points A and C can be moved farther apart, thereby increasing the length of AC and therefore the area of the trapezoid.

If your choice was
(A, B, or C), see the solution above.

10. (D) Let AB = DC = b (where b represents the base of both $\triangle$ABE and $\triangle$DEC). Let AD = BC = x, and h equal the height of $\triangle$AEB. Then the height of $\triangle$DEC will be $x - h$.

The area of $\triangle$AEB = $\frac{1}{2}bh$ and the area of $\triangle$DEC = $\frac{1}{2}b(x - h)$.

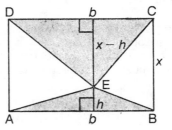

Therefore,
$$\text{Area of shaded part} = \text{Area of } \triangle\text{AEB} + \text{Area of } \triangle\text{DEC}$$
$$= \tfrac{1}{2}bh + \tfrac{1}{2}b(x - h)$$
$$= \tfrac{1}{2}bh + \tfrac{1}{2}bx - \tfrac{1}{2}bh$$
$$= \tfrac{1}{2}bx$$

Thus, the sum does not depend on the position of point E.

If your choice was
(A, B, or C), see the solution above.

11. (B) The four triangles formed are 30-60-90 triangles.
Therefore, AB = $4\sqrt{3}$. In the smaller triangle, CD = $2\sqrt{3}$.

Thus, AB + CD = $4\sqrt{3} + 2\sqrt{3} = 6\sqrt{3}$.

If your choice was
(A), you used the relationships for a 45-45-90 triangle.
(C), you incorrectly combined $\sqrt{3} + \sqrt{3}$ as $\sqrt{6}$.
(D), you combined the two square roots of 3 as 3 and then multiplied by 4 + 2 or 6.

12. (D) The piece of wire is $2\pi \cdot 14 = 2 \cdot \frac{\overset{2}{\cancel{22}}}{\cancel{7}_1} \cdot \cancel{14}$ or 88 cm long.

Therefore, a side of the square is $\frac{88}{4}$ or 22 cm long. The area of the square is 22^2 or 484 square centimeters.

If your choice was
(A), you found the area of a circle of radius 7.
(B), you found the area of a circle of radius 14.
(C), you mistook the circumference of the circle for the area.

13. (C) Eight units below point A along the y-axis is $(0, -2)$. Two units to the left on a line parallel to the x-axis is point $B(-2, -2)$.

Apply the Pythagorean theorem.
$$(AB)^2 = 8^2 + 2^2$$
$$(AB)^2 = 64 + 4 = 68$$
$$AB = \sqrt{68}$$

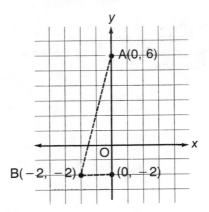

If your choice was
(A), you thought $\overline{AB}$ was a leg of the right triangle.
(B), you found $8^2 = 64$ but you squared 2 as 2.
(D), you forgot to take the square root of 68.

14. (C) Since the measure of angle O is 30°, the area of each sector OCD and OAB is $\frac{30}{360}$ or $\frac{1}{12}$ of the area of the circle with the same radius.

Area of sector OCD $= \frac{1}{12}\pi 2^2 = \frac{\pi}{3}$

Area of sector OAB $= \frac{1}{12}\pi 4^2 = \frac{4}{3}\pi$

$$\begin{array}{ccc} \text{Area of} \\ \text{shaded region} \end{array} = \begin{array}{c} \text{Area of} \\ \text{sector OAB} \end{array} - \begin{array}{c} \text{Area of} \\ \text{sector OCD} \end{array}$$

$$= \frac{4}{3}\pi - \frac{\pi}{3}$$

$$= \pi$$

If your choice was
(A), you found the area of sector OCD.
(B), you found one half the area of sector OAB.
(D), you found the area of sector OAB.

15. **(A)** The sum of the degree measures of a quadrilateral is 360. Therefore, the fourth angle of the quadrilateral can be written as $360 - 3x$.

Since each angle is less than $120°$, then
$$360 - 3x < 120$$
$$240 < 3x$$
$$80 < x \quad \text{or} \quad x > 80$$

If your choice was
(B or C), see the solution above.
(D), the figure might be a square but the question says "must be true."

Part Four

Two SAT-Type Geometry Tests

This section contains two SAT-Type Geometry Tests modeled after the SAT Mathematics Section.

Use the Answer Sheet that precedes each test to record your answers. The Answer Sheet for Test 1 is found on page 140. The Answer Sheet for Test 2 is on page 154.

After you have completed each test, you can check your answers using the Answer Keys on pages 146 and 160. If you need additional help, each answer is referenced (in parentheses) to the appropriate Geometry Refresher Section.

The solutions with error analysis begin on page 147 and on page 161.

Types of Multiple-Choice Questions

There are two types of multiple-choice questions used in the mathematics section of the SAT: the standard multiple-choice questions and quantitative comparison questions. There are approximately twice as many standard multiple-choice questions as quantitative comparison questions on the test.

Reference Information for SAT-Type Tests

In the introduction to each section of the SAT math test, information is provided for your reference in solving some of the problems. This information appears in the test booklet. Knowledge of this information beforehand will help when you take the actual test. (See inside back cover.)

Answer Sheet*

SAT-Type Geometry Test 1

1. (A) (B) (C) (D) (E)
2. (A) (B) (C) (D) (E)
3. (A) (B) (C) (D) (E)
4. (A) (B) (C) (D) (E)
5. (A) (B) (C) (D) (E)
6. (A) (B) (C) (D) (E)
7. (A) (B) (C) (D) (E)
8. (A) (B) (C) (D) (E)
9. (A) (B) (C) (D) (E)
10. (A) (B) (C) (D) (E)
11. (A) (B) (C) (D) (E)
12. (A) (B) (C) (D) (E)
13. (A) (B) (C) (D) (E)
14. (A) (B) (C) (D) (E)
15. (A) (B) (C) (D) (E)

16. (A) (B) (C) (D) (E)
17. (A) (B) (C) (D) (E)
18. (A) (B) (C) (D) (E)
19. (A) (B) (C) (D) (E)
20. (A) (B) (C) (D) (E)
21. (A) (B) (C) (D) (E)
22. (A) (B) (C) (D) (E)
23. (A) (B) (C) (D) (E)
24. (A) (B) (C) (D) (E)
25. (A) (B) (C) (D) (E)
26. (A) (B) (C) (D) (E)
27. (A) (B) (C) (D) (E)
28. (A) (B) (C) (D) (E)
29. (A) (B) (C) (D) (E)
30. (A) (B) (C) (D) (E)

*An Answer Sheet very much like this will be given to you at the actual test. In doing the following practice test, you may wish to record your answers on this Answer Sheet. However, it may be more convenient for you to circle your answer from among the choices provided.

SAT-Type Geometry Test 1

Directions:
Solve each problem in this practice test. Use any available space on the page for scratchwork. Then decide which is the best of the choices given and either darken the corresponding space on the Answer Sheet on page 140 or circle your answer from among the choices provided.

1. In the figure at the right, if $\overrightarrow{DE} \perp \overrightarrow{DB}$, then $x =$

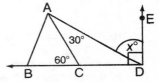

   (A) 30   (B) 45   (C) 60
   (D) 75   (E) 90

2. Which of the following figures can be drawn without lifting the pencil or retracing a segment?

   I.   II.   III.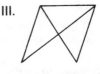

   (A) I only   (B) II only   (C) III only
   (D) I and II only   (E) I and III only

3. In the figure at the right, the coordinates of point P are (4, 4). If point P is rotated 90° to the left to point P′, what are the coordinates of point P′?

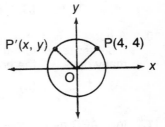

   (A) $(-4, -4)$ (B) $(4, -4)$
   (C) $(-4, 4)$ (D) $(4, 4)$
   (E) It cannot be determined from the information given.

4. In the figure at the right, if the large circle has radius r and the small circle has diameter r, then the ratio of the area of the shaded region to the area of the small circle is

   (A) 16 : 3   (B) 4 : 1   (C) 8 : 3
   (D) 3 : 1   (E) 2 : 1

5. L, M, N, and P are four distinct lines in a plane. If $L \perp M$, $N \parallel L$, and $P \parallel L$, then all of the following are false EXCEPT

   (A) $P \perp N$ (B) $P \parallel M$ (C) $L \perp P$
   (D) $M \parallel N$ (E) $P \perp M$

6. In the figure at the right, $\overline{AB}$, $\overline{BC}$, and $\overline{CA}$ are tangent to the circle at D, E, and F respectively. If AD = 3, BE = 5, and CF = 7, then $a + b + c =$

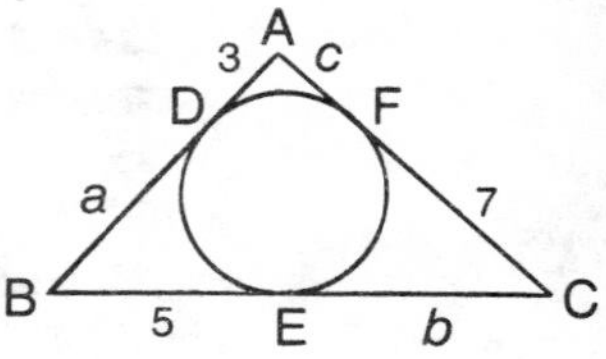

(A) $7\frac{1}{2}$ (B) 10   (C) 15

(D) 18   (E) 30

7. In rectangle ABCD at the right, BC = 16 and $\overline{EF} \perp \overline{AB}$. If EG = 10 and EJ = 12, then HF =

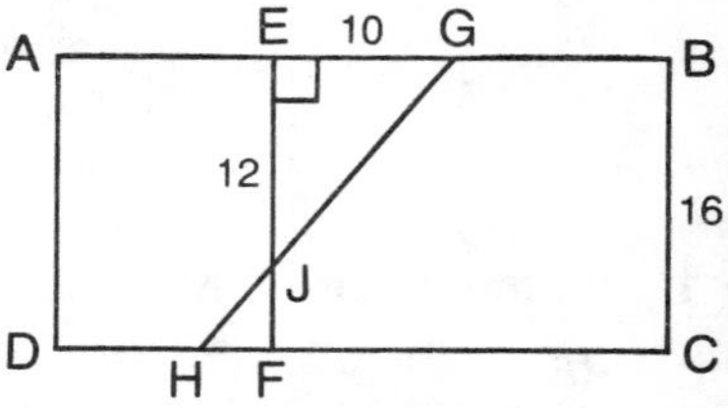

(A) 3   (B) $3\frac{1}{3}$

(C) $3\frac{1}{2}$ (D) 4

(E) It cannot be determined from the information given.

8. In the diagram at the right, the area of the shaded region is

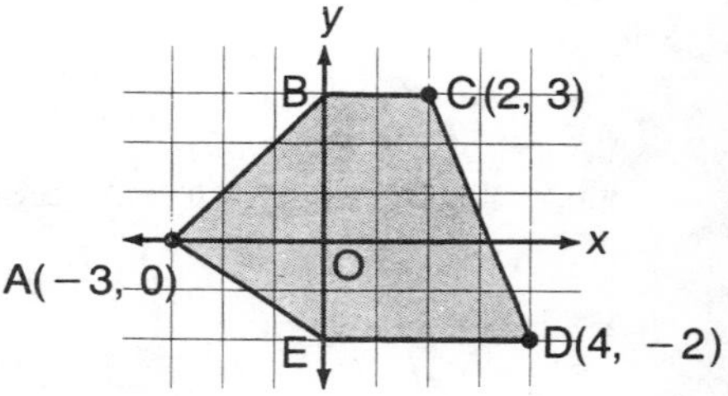

(A) 22   (B) $22\frac{1}{2}$

(C) 23   (D) 25

(E) It cannot be any of the above numbers.

9. If the average of the degree measures of two angles of an *isosceles* triangle is 65, which of the following could be the degree measure of one of the angles of the triangle?

(A) 40   (B) 60   (C) 70   (D) 80   (E) 100

10. A horse is tied to a stake in the middle of a pasture with a 7-foot rope. If the horse eats 80 square feet of grass a day, for how many days will the horse have enough to eat?

(A) 1   (B) 2   (C) 3   (D) 4   (E) 5

11. In $\triangle ABC$ at the right, if AB > CB > AC, then

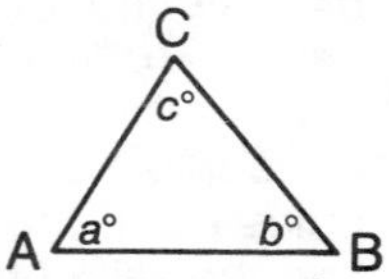

(A) $b > a$ (B) $b > c$ (C) $a > c$
(D) $b > 60$ (E) $c > 60$

12. If a rectangular prism has length 5, width 2, and height 4, then the total surface area is

(A) 40   (B) 56   (C) 66   (D) 68   (E) 76

13. In the triangle at the right, what is the value of z in terms of x?

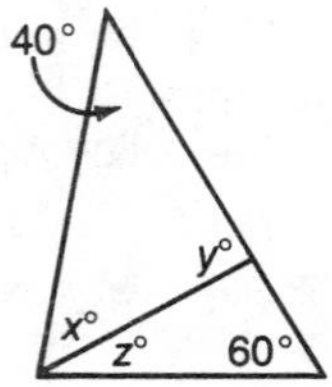

(A) $2x$ (B) $x - 40$ (C) $x - 20$
(D) $80 - x$ (E) $100 - x$

14. A leg of a right triangle is 4. Find the other leg if the area of the triangle is equal to the area of the circle drawn at the right.

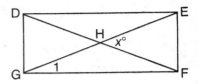

(A) 1π (B) 2π (C) 3π
(D) 4π (E) 5π

15. In rectangle DEFG at the right, if $m\angle 1 = 22°$, then $x =$

(A) 22   (B) 33
(C) 44   (D) 68
(E) 136

16. The diameter of a circle whose area is 36 is

(A) $\frac{6}{\sqrt{\pi}}$ (B) $\sqrt{\frac{12}{\pi}}$ (C) $\sqrt{\frac{6}{\pi}}$ (D) $\frac{12}{\sqrt{\pi}}$ (E) $\frac{\sqrt{\pi}}{3}$

Questions 17-26 each consist of two quantities, one in Column A and one in Column B. You are to compare the two quantities and on the answer sheet blacken space

    A if the quantity in Column A is greater;
    B if the quantity in Column B is greater;
    C if the two quantities are equal;
    D if the relationship cannot be determined from the information given.

An E response will not be scored.

Notes:
1. In certain questions, information concerning one or both of the quantities to be compared is centered above the two columns.
2. In a given question, a symbol that appears in both columns represents the same thing in Column A as it does in Column B.
3. Letters such as *x, n,* and *k* stand for real numbers.

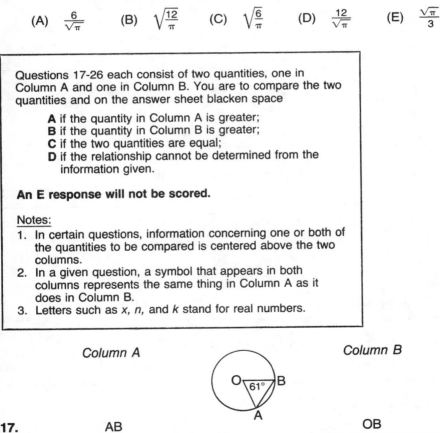

Column A   *Column B*

17.   AB   OB

A triangle with sides *m, m* + 2, and *m* + 3.

18. The number of triangles   0
        with *m* = 1

143

	Column A	Column B

19. The area of a rhombus with perimeter 20   The area of a square with perimeter 16

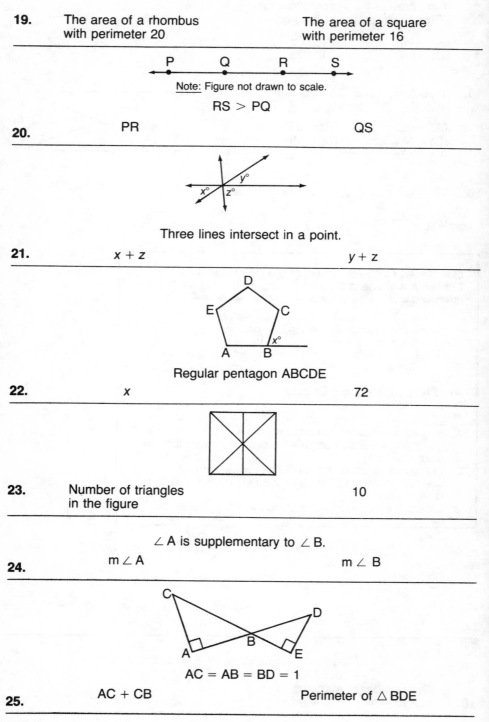

Note: Figure not drawn to scale.

RS > PQ

20.   PR   QS

Three lines intersect in a point.

21. $x + z$ $y + z$

Regular pentagon ABCDE

22. x 72

23. Number of triangles in the figure   10

∠ A is supplementary to ∠ B.

24.   m ∠ A   m ∠ B

AC = AB = BD = 1

25.   AC + CB   Perimeter of △ BDE

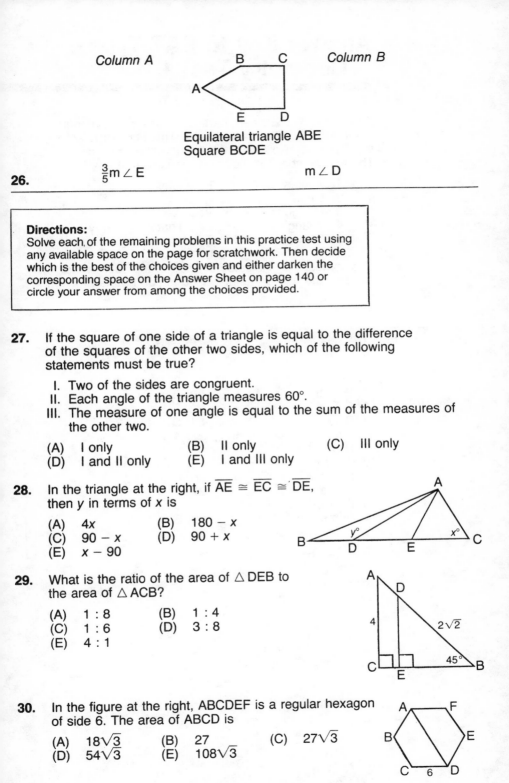

Column A   Column B

Equilateral triangle ABE
Square BCDE

26. $\frac{3}{5}$m ∠ E   m ∠ D

Directions:
Solve each. of the remaining problems in this practice test using any available space on the page for scratchwork. Then decide which is the best of the choices given and either darken the corresponding space on the Answer Sheet on page 140 or circle your answer from among the choices provided.

27. If the square of one side of a triangle is equal to the difference of the squares of the other two sides, which of the following statements must be true?

   I. Two of the sides are congruent.
   II. Each angle of the triangle measures 60°.
   III. The measure of one angle is equal to the sum of the measures of the other two.

   (A) I only   (B) II only   (C) III only
   (D) I and II only   (E) I and III only

28. In the triangle at the right, if $\overline{AE} \cong \overline{EC} \cong \overline{DE}$, then y in terms of x is

   (A) $4x$ (B) $180 - x$
   (C) $90 - x$ (D) $90 + x$
   (E) $x - 90$

29. What is the ratio of the area of $\triangle DEB$ to the area of $\triangle ACB$?

   (A) 1 : 8   (B) 1 : 4
   (C) 1 : 6   (D) 3 : 8
   (E) 4 : 1

30. In the figure at the right, ABCDEF is a regular hexagon of side 6. The area of ABCD is

   (A) $18\sqrt{3}$ (B) 27   (C) $27\sqrt{3}$
   (D) $54\sqrt{3}$ (E) $108\sqrt{3}$

Answer Key to SAT-Type Geometry Test 1

Following each answer, there is a number or numbers in the form "*a.b*" in parentheses. This number refers to the Geometry Refresher Section (beginning on page 23). The first number "*a*" indicates the section.

1. Angles	6. Perimeter
2. Lines	7. Area
3. Polygons	8. Volume
4. Triangles	9. Coordinate Geometry
5. Circles	10. Problem Solving

The number "*b*" indicates the part of the section that explains the rule or method used in solving the problem.

1. C (4.6, 2.4)	**16.** D (7.6, 5.1)
2. E (2.1)	**17.** A (4.5, 4.3, 4.7)
3. C (9.5)	**18.** C (4.7)
4. D (7.6)	**19.** D (6.3, 7.1, 7.3)
5. E (2.8)	**20.** B (2.1, 4.7)
6. C (5.4)	**21.** C (1.9)
7. B (3.6, 3.5)	**22.** C (3.3)
8. B (9.5, 7.5, 7.4)	**23.** A (3.6)
9. D (4.5, 4.3)	**24.** D (1.8)
10. A (7.6)	**25.** C (4.8, 6.2)
11. E (4.7, 4.3)	**26.** C (4.3, 3.6)
12. E (7.8)	**27.** C (4.8)
13. D (4.3)	**28.** D (4.5, 4.6, 4.3)
14. B (7.5, 7.6)	**29.** B (4.8, 7.5)
15. C (3.6, 4.5, 4.6)	**30.** C (7.7)

Solutions for
SAT-Type Geometry Test 1

1. (C) $\angle$ ACB is an exterior angle of $\triangle$ ACD. The measure of an exterior angle of a triangle is equal to the sum of the measures of the nonadjacent interior angles of the triangle.

$$m \angle ACB = 30° + m \angle CDA$$
$$60° = 30° + m \angle CDA$$
$$30° = m \angle CDA$$

Thus,
$$m \angle CDE = m \angle CDA + m \angle ADE$$
$$90° = 30° + x°$$
$$60 = x$$

2. (E) In attempting to draw all three figures, only figures I and III can be done. The diagrams below show one possible way of drawing each figure.

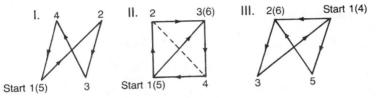

I.   4   2   II. 2   3(6)   III. 2(6)   Start 1(4)

Start 1(5)   3   Start 1(5)   4   3   5

3. (C) Draw line segment PP′. $\overline{OPP′}$ is a right isosceles triangle with the y-axis bisecting $\overline{PP′}$. The y-axis is a line of symmetry and P and P′ are reflections of each other. Thus, if point P has coordinates (4, 4), then P′ has coordinates (-4, 4).

4. (D) Use the following relationship:

Area of shaded = Area of large $-$ Area of small
region   circle   circle

$$= \pi r^2 - \pi \left(\frac{r}{2}\right)^2$$

$$= \pi r^2 - \frac{\pi r^2}{4} = \frac{3\pi r^2}{4}$$

Thus, $\dfrac{\text{Area of shaded region}}{\text{Area of small circle}} = \dfrac{\frac{3\pi r^2}{4}}{\frac{\pi r^2}{4}}$

$$= \frac{3\cancel{\pi r^2}}{\cancel{4}} \times \frac{\cancel{4}}{\cancel{\pi r^2}} = \frac{3}{1}$$

5. (E) Draw a diagram to show that P $\perp$ M is the only true statement.

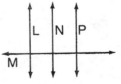

L   N   P

M

6. (C) The tangent segments to a circle from a point outside the circle are congruent, so $AD = c$, $BE = a$, and $FC = b$. Thus, $a + b + c = 5 + 7 + 3 = 15$.

7. (B) Since EBCF is a rectangle, $\overline{EF} \cong \overline{BC}$ and $BC = EJ + JF$. Therefore $JF = 4$. Since $\triangle JEG \sim \triangle JFH$, write the following proportion:

$$\frac{HF}{10} = \frac{4}{12}$$

In a proportion, the product of the extremes is equal to the product of the means.

$$12(HF) = 40$$
$$HF = 3\tfrac{1}{3}$$

8. (B) Since the coordinates of point C are $(2, 3)$ and of point D are $(4, -2)$, it can be found that point B is $(0, 3)$ and point E is $(0, -2)$.

The area of the shaded region is the sum of the areas of $\triangle ABE$ and trapezoid BCDE.

Area of $\triangle ABE$:　　$A = \tfrac{1}{2}bh$

$$A = \tfrac{1}{2}(BE)(AO)$$
$$A = \tfrac{1}{2}(5)(3) = 7\tfrac{1}{2}$$

Area of trapezoid BCDE:　$A = \tfrac{1}{2}h(b_1 + b_2)$

$$A = \tfrac{1}{2}(BE)(BC + ED)$$
$$A = \tfrac{1}{2}(5)(2 + 4)$$
$$A = \tfrac{1}{2}(5)(6) = 15$$

Thus, the area of $ABCDE = 15 + 7\tfrac{1}{2} = 22\tfrac{1}{2}$.

9. (D) The two angles whose average degree measure is 65 could be the congruent base angles or the noncongruent angles. Consider each case separately.

Case I

$$\frac{a + a}{2} = 65$$
$$2a = 130$$
$$a = 65$$

$$2a + b = 180$$
$$2(65) + b = 180$$
$$130 + b = 180$$
$$b = 50$$

65°, 65°, 50°

Case II

$$\frac{a + b}{2} = 65$$
$$a + b = 130$$
$$a + a + b = 180$$
$$a + 130 = 180$$
$$a = 50$$

$$a + b = 130$$
$$50 + b = 130$$
$$b = 80$$

50°, 50°, 80°

10. (A) The horse can move about and eat grass inside a circle of radius 7 feet. The area of this circle is

$$A = \pi r^2$$
$$A = \left(\frac{22}{7}\right)7^2$$
$$A = 154 \text{ ft}^2$$

Since the horse eats 80 ft^2 of grass a day, the horse will have enough grass for 1 day.

11. (E) If the measures of two sides of a triangle are unequal, the measures of the angles opposite these sides are unequal in the same order.
Thus, if $AB > CB > AC$, then $c > a > b$. It follows from $a + b + c = 180$ and $c > a > b$ that $c > 60$.

12. (E) The side face has an area of $4 \times 2 = 8$, the front face has an area of $5 \times 4 = 20$, and the bottom face has an area of $5 \times 2 = 10$. The sum is $8 + 20 + 10 = 38$. Each face has a congruent face opposite it, so the total surface area is $2(38) = 76$.

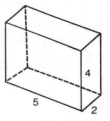

13. (D) The sum of the degree measures of the angles of a triangle is 180 so

$$x + z + 40 + 60 = 180$$
$$x + z + 100 = 180$$
$$x + z = 80$$
$$z = 80 - x$$

14. (B) The area of the circle is $A = \pi r^2$.
$$A = \pi(2)^2$$
$$A = 4\pi$$

The area of a right triangle is equal to one half the product of the lengths of the two legs, so

$$A = \frac{1}{2}\ell_1\ell_2$$
$$A = \frac{1}{2}(4)\ell_2 = 2\ell_2$$

Since the areas of the right triangle and the circle are equal, it follows that

$$4\pi = 2\ell_2$$
$$2\pi = \ell_2$$

15. (C) Since the diagonals of a rectangle are congruent and bisect each other, it follows that $\overline{GH} \cong \overline{DH} \cong \overline{HE} \cong \overline{HF}$. If $\overline{GH} \cong \overline{HF}$, then $\angle 1 \cong \angle GFH$, and exterior angle x is equal to $m\angle 1 + m\angle GFH$. Thus, $m\angle x = 44°$.

16. (D) The area of a circle is $A = \pi r^2$.

$$36 = \pi r^2$$
$$\frac{36}{\pi} = r^2$$
$$\frac{6}{\sqrt{\pi}} = r$$

Thus, the diameter is $2\left(\frac{6}{\sqrt{\pi}}\right) = \frac{12}{\sqrt{\pi}}$.

17. (A) OAB is an isosceles triangle with $\overline{OA} \cong \overline{OB}$, and $m \angle OAB = m \angle OBA = x°$. Since the sum of the measures of the angles in a triangle is $180°$,

$$m \angle AOB + m \angle OAB + m \angle OBA = 180°.$$
$$61 + x + x = 180$$
$$2x = 119$$
$$x = 59\frac{1}{2}$$

But, if the measures of two angles of a triangle are unequal, the measures of the sides opposite these angles are unequal in the same order.
Thus, AB > OB.

18. (C) If $m = 1$, the sides of the triangle measure 1, 1 + 2, and 1 + 3, or 1, 3, and 4. These values cannot represent the sides of a triangle since 1 + 3 = 4, and the sum of the measures of two sides of a triangle must always be greater than the measure of the third side.

19. (D) Use the formulas for a square.

$$P = 4s \qquad A = s^2$$
$$16 = 4s \qquad A = 4^2$$
$$4 = s \qquad A = 16$$

The perimeter of a rhombus is 20 and each side is 5. If the least distance from a point to a line is the measure of the segment from that point perpendicular to the line, then $h < 5$.

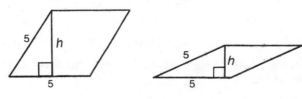

Let $h = 4$
$A = bh$
$A = 5(4)$
$A = 20$

Let $h = 2$
$A = bh$
$A = 5(2)$
$A = 10$

Thus, 20 > 16 but 16 > 10.

20. (B) If equals are added to unequals, the sum is unequal in the same order.

$$RS > PQ$$
$$QR = QR$$
$$RS + QR > PQ + QR$$
$$QS > PR$$

21. (C) Since vertical angles are congruent, $x = y$. By the addition axiom for real numbers, if $x = y$, then $x + z = y + z$.

22. (C) The measure of an exterior angle of a regular polygon is $360°$ divided by the number of sides n.

Therefore, $\frac{360°}{5} = 72°$ and $x = 72$.

23. (A) The diagonals divide the square into four different half squares, and four different quarter squares. Two quarter triangles are divided by the vertical line into four eighth triangles, making 12 triangles in all.

24. (D) If $\angle A$ is supplementary to $\angle B$, then $m \angle A + m \angle B = 180°$. Since there is more than one pair of numbers whose sum is 180, the relationship cannot be determined.

25. (C) ABC and BDE are 45-45-90 triangles. Since the measure of the hypotenuse is equal to the product of the measure of one of the equal legs and $\sqrt{2}$, $BC = (1)(\sqrt{2})$ or $\sqrt{2}$.

In $\triangle BDE$, the measure of either leg is equal to the product of $\frac{1}{2}$ the measure of the hypotenuse and $\sqrt{2}$.

Therefore, $BE = ED = \frac{1}{2}(1)(\sqrt{2}) = \frac{\sqrt{2}}{2}$.

Thus, $AC + CB = 1 + \sqrt{2}$ and the perimeter of $\triangle BDE$ is $1 + \frac{\sqrt{2}}{2} + \frac{\sqrt{2}}{2} = 1 + \sqrt{2}$.

26. (C) $\angle E$ is made up by one angle of the triangle plus one angle of the square, so $m \angle E = 60° + 90° = 150°$.

Since $m \angle D = 90°$, and $\frac{3}{5}(150°) = 90°$, it follows that $\frac{3}{5}m \angle E = m \angle D$.

27. (C) In the diagram below, $x^2 = z^2 - y^2$ or $x^2 + y^2 = z^2$. But if the sum of the measures of two sides of a triangle is equal to the square of the measure of the third side, the triangle is a right triangle. Therefore, XYZ is a right triangle with $m \angle Z = 90°$.

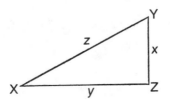

Since $m \angle X + m \angle Y = 90°$, $m \angle X + m \angle Y = m \angle Z$.

If your choice was

(A), you assumed that the relationship is true for an isosceles triangle. If the sides are designated by *a, a,* and *b,* then there are three possibilities:

$a^2 = a^2 - b^2$ or $b = 0$ (Impossible)

$b^2 = a^2 - a^2$ or $b = 0$ (Impossible)

$a^2 = b^2 - a^2$ or $b = a\sqrt{2}$ (Right Isosceles Triangle)

(B), you assumed that the triangle is equilateral. If each side is *a,* then $a^2 = a^2 - a^2$ or $a = 0$.

(D), see (A) and (B) above.

(E), see (A) above.

28. (D) ACE is an isosceles triangle with $m \angle A = m \angle C = x$. AED is an exterior angle of $\triangle$ AEC and is $2x$, since the measure of an exterior angle of a triangle is equal to the sum of the measures of the nonadjacent angles of the triangle.

AED is an isosceles triangle with $m \angle DAE = m \angle ADE$. If $m \angle AED = 2x$, then $m \angle DAE + m \angle ADE = 180 - 2x$.

Since $m \angle DAE = m \angle ADE$, $2m \angle DAE = 180 - 2x$, and $m \angle DAE = 90 - x$. $\angle ADB$ is an exterior angle of $\triangle$ ADE, so $m \angle ADB = m \angle DAE + m \angle AED$

$$y = (90 - x) + 2x$$
$$y = 90 + x$$

If your choice was

(A), you found $m \angle AED = m \angle DAE = 2x$.

(B), you found $m \angle AEC = 2x$, so $m \angle ADE = x$.

(C), you found the measure of $\angle ADE$ instead of its supplement $\angle ADB$.

(E), you incorrectly solved $y - x = 90$ as $y = x - 90$.

29. (B) Both DEB and ACB are 45-45-90 triangles. Use this relationship:

$$DE = EB = \frac{1}{2}(DB)\sqrt{2}$$

$$DE = EB = \frac{1}{\cancel{2}} (\cancel{2}\sqrt{2})\sqrt{2}$$

$$DE = EB = 2$$

In isosceles $\triangle$ ACB, CB = 4.

Thus,

$$\text{Area of } \triangle DEB = \frac{1}{\cancel{2}}(\cancel{2})(2) = 2$$

$$\text{Area of } \triangle ACB = \frac{1}{\cancel{2}}(\cancel{4})(4) = 8$$

$$\frac{\text{Area of } \triangle DEB}{\text{Area of } \triangle ACB} = \frac{2}{8} = \frac{1}{4}$$

If your choice was
(A), you forgot to multiply the area of $\triangle ACB$ by one half.
(C), you found $CE = 4$ and $CB = 6$.
(D), you found $DE = EB = \sqrt{6}$ by applying the 30-60-90 triangle theorem to $\triangle DEB$.
(E), you found the inverse ratio.

30. (C) If A = area, a = length of the apothem, and p = perimeter, the area of a regular polygon is

$$A = \tfrac{1}{2}ap$$

When the apothem is drawn to the side of a regular hexagon, a 30-60-90 triangle is formed. The length of the apothem is $3\sqrt{3}$. and the perimeter is 36, so

$$A = \tfrac{1}{2}(3\sqrt{3})(36)$$
$$A = 54\sqrt{3}$$

Thus, the area of ABCD $= \tfrac{1}{2}(54\sqrt{3}) = 27\sqrt{3}$.

If your choice was
(A), you thought the area of ABCD was one third the area of ABCDEF.
(B), you forgot to include $\sqrt{3}$ in the answer.
(D), you found the area of the entire regular hexagon.
(E), you wrote the formula as $A = ap$.

Answer Sheet*

SAT-Type Geometry Test 2

1. Ⓐ Ⓑ Ⓒ Ⓓ Ⓔ   16. Ⓐ Ⓑ Ⓒ Ⓓ Ⓔ
2. Ⓐ Ⓑ Ⓒ Ⓓ Ⓔ   17. Ⓐ Ⓑ Ⓒ Ⓓ Ⓔ
3. Ⓐ Ⓑ Ⓒ Ⓓ Ⓔ   18. Ⓐ Ⓑ Ⓒ Ⓓ Ⓔ
4. Ⓐ Ⓑ Ⓒ Ⓓ Ⓔ   19. Ⓐ Ⓑ Ⓒ Ⓓ Ⓔ
5. Ⓐ Ⓑ Ⓒ Ⓓ Ⓔ   20. Ⓐ Ⓑ Ⓒ Ⓓ Ⓔ
6. Ⓐ Ⓑ Ⓒ Ⓓ Ⓔ   21. Ⓐ Ⓑ Ⓒ Ⓓ Ⓔ
7. Ⓐ Ⓑ Ⓒ Ⓓ Ⓔ   22. Ⓐ Ⓑ Ⓒ Ⓓ Ⓔ
8. Ⓐ Ⓑ Ⓒ Ⓓ Ⓔ   23. Ⓐ Ⓑ Ⓒ Ⓓ Ⓔ
9. Ⓐ Ⓑ Ⓒ Ⓓ Ⓔ   24. Ⓐ Ⓑ Ⓒ Ⓓ Ⓔ
10. Ⓐ Ⓑ Ⓒ Ⓓ Ⓔ   25. Ⓐ Ⓑ Ⓒ Ⓓ Ⓔ
11. Ⓐ Ⓑ Ⓒ Ⓓ Ⓔ   26. Ⓐ Ⓑ Ⓒ Ⓓ Ⓔ
12. Ⓐ Ⓑ Ⓒ Ⓓ Ⓔ   27. Ⓐ Ⓑ Ⓒ Ⓓ Ⓔ
13. Ⓐ Ⓑ Ⓒ Ⓓ Ⓔ   28. Ⓐ Ⓑ Ⓒ Ⓓ Ⓔ
14. Ⓐ Ⓑ Ⓒ Ⓓ Ⓔ   29. Ⓐ Ⓑ Ⓒ Ⓓ Ⓔ
15. Ⓐ Ⓑ Ⓒ Ⓓ Ⓔ   30. Ⓐ Ⓑ Ⓒ Ⓓ Ⓔ

*An Answer Sheet very much like this will be given to you at the actual test. In doing the following practice test, you may wish to record your answers on this Answer Sheet. However, it may be more convenient for you to circle your answer from among the choices provided.

SAT-Type Geometry Test 2

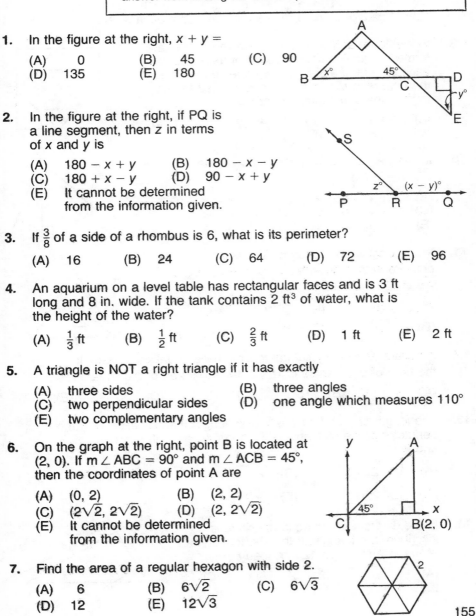

1. In the figure at the right, $x + y =$

    (A)   0   (B)   45   (C)   90
    (D)   135   (E)   180

2. In the figure at the right, if PQ is a line segment, then z in terms of x and y is

    (A) $180 - x + y$ (B) $180 - x - y$
    (C) $180 + x - y$ (D) $90 - x + y$
    (E)   It cannot be determined from the information given.

3. If $\frac{3}{8}$ of a side of a rhombus is 6, what is its perimeter?

    (A)   16   (B)   24   (C)   64   (D)   72   (E)   96

4. An aquarium on a level table has rectangular faces and is 3 ft long and 8 in. wide. If the tank contains 2 ft^3 of water, what is the height of the water?

    (A) $\frac{1}{3}$ ft   (B) $\frac{1}{2}$ ft   (C) $\frac{2}{3}$ ft   (D)   1 ft   (E)   2 ft

5. A triangle is NOT a right triangle if it has exactly

    (A)   three sides   (B)   three angles
    (C)   two perpendicular sides   (D)   one angle which measures 110°
    (E)   two complementary angles

6. On the graph at the right, point B is located at (2, 0). If m $\angle$ ABC = 90° and m $\angle$ ACB = 45°, then the coordinates of point A are

    (A)   (0, 2)   (B)   (2, 2)
    (C) $(2\sqrt{2}, 2\sqrt{2})$ (D) $(2, 2\sqrt{2})$
    (E)   It cannot be determined from the information given.

7. Find the area of a regular hexagon with side 2.

    (A)   6   (B) $6\sqrt{2}$ (C) $6\sqrt{3}$
    (D)   12   (E) $12\sqrt{3}$

155

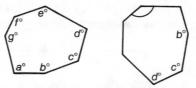

8. If the figure at the left above is moved to the position indicated by the angle measurements in the figure at the right above, what is the measure of the marked angle?

(A) $a°$ (B) $e°$ (C) $f°$ (D) $g°$

(E) It cannot be determined from the information given.

9. In the figure at the right, successive squares are formed by joining the midpoints of the sides of each square. If a side of the large square is 2, then the ratio of the area of the shaded region to the area of the large square is

(A) 1 : 8   (B) 1 : 4   (C) 1 : 3

(D) 3 : 8   (E) 1 : 2

10. In the diagram at the right, if $b > a$ and $\overline{CD} \perp \overline{AB}$, then

(A) $x + y = b - a$ (B) $x + y = a + b$

(C) $x - y = a + b$ (D) $x - y = a - b$

(E) $x - y = b - a$

11. In the diagram at the right, ABC is an equilateral triangle with side 8. If $\overline{AD} \perp \overline{BC}$ and $\overline{AE} \cong \overline{ED}$, then BE =

(A) $\sqrt{20}$ (B) $\frac{8}{3}\sqrt{3}$ (C) $\sqrt{28}$

(D) $\sqrt{63}$ (E) 8

12. A square and an equilateral triangle have equal perimeters. If the area of the triangle is $16\sqrt{3}$, then the area of the square is

(A) 9   (B) 16   (C) 25   (D) 36   (E) 576

13. The length of a rectangle is x units longer than its width w. If the perimeter of the rectangle is P, then the value of x in terms of P and w is

(A) $\frac{P}{2} - 2w$ (B) $P - 2w$ (C) $\frac{P}{2} - 4w$

(D) $\frac{P}{2} + 2w$ (E) $P + 2w$

14. In the diagram at the right, the circle is inscribed in a triangle. If the shorter segment of the side of length 12 is r, then $r =$

(A) 1   (B) 2   (C) 3

(D) 4   (E) 5

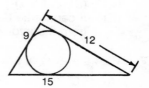

15. In the diagram at the right, △ ABC and △ BCD are equilateral with a common base $\overline{BC}$ and line segment $\overline{AD}$. Which of the following statements must be true?

I. $\overline{AD} \perp \overline{BC}$
II. $AB : CD = AC : BD$
III. $\angle ACB \cong \angle CBD$

(A) I only
(B) II only
(C) III only
(D) I and III only
(E) I, II, and III

16. In the diagram at the right, if $\ell_1 \parallel \ell_2$ and $\overline{AB} \cong \overline{CD}$, then

(A) $\overline{AE} \cong \overline{EC}$
(B) $\overline{AD} \cong \overline{BC}$
(C) $\overline{AC} \cong \overline{BD}$
(D) $\overline{AD} \perp \overline{BC}$
(E) It cannot be determined from the information given.

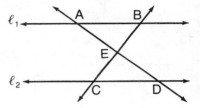

Questions 17–26 each consist of two quantities, one in Column A and one in Column B. You are to compare the two quantities and on the answer sheet blacken space

A if the quantity in Column A is greater;
B if the quantity in Column B is greater;
C if the two quantities are equal;
D if the relationship cannot be determined from the information given.

An E response will not be scored.

Notes:
1. In certain questions, information concerning one or both of the quantities to be compared is centered above the two columns.
2. In a given response, a symbol that appears in both columns represents the same thing in Column A as it does in Column B.
3. Letters such as *x, n,* and *k* stand for real numbers.

Column A   *Column B*

Trapezoid ABCD with bases BC and AD.
Angles BAD and CDA are congruent.

17.   BC   AD

	Column A	Column B

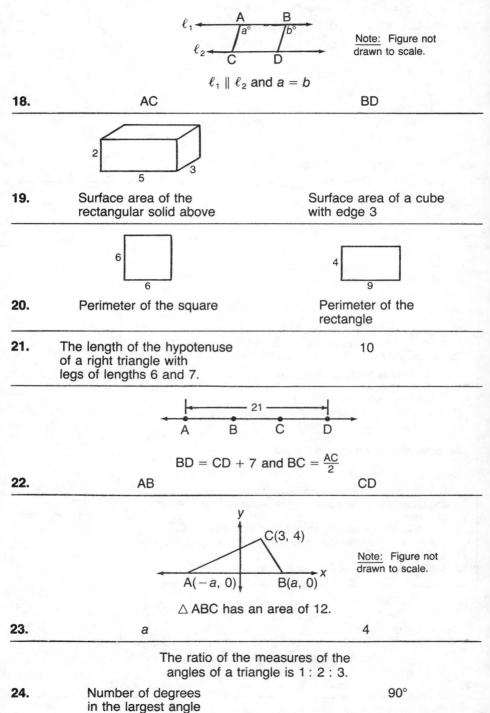

$\ell_1 \parallel \ell_2$ and $a = b$

18.   AC   BD

Note: Figure not drawn to scale.

19. Surface area of the rectangular solid above   Surface area of a cube with edge 3

20. Perimeter of the square   Perimeter of the rectangle

21. The length of the hypotenuse of a right triangle with legs of lengths 6 and 7.   10

$BD = CD + 7$ and $BC = \frac{AC}{2}$

22.   AB   CD

$\triangle ABC$ has an area of 12.

Note: Figure not drawn to scale.

23. a 4

The ratio of the measures of the angles of a triangle is 1 : 2 : 3.

24. Number of degrees in the largest angle   90°

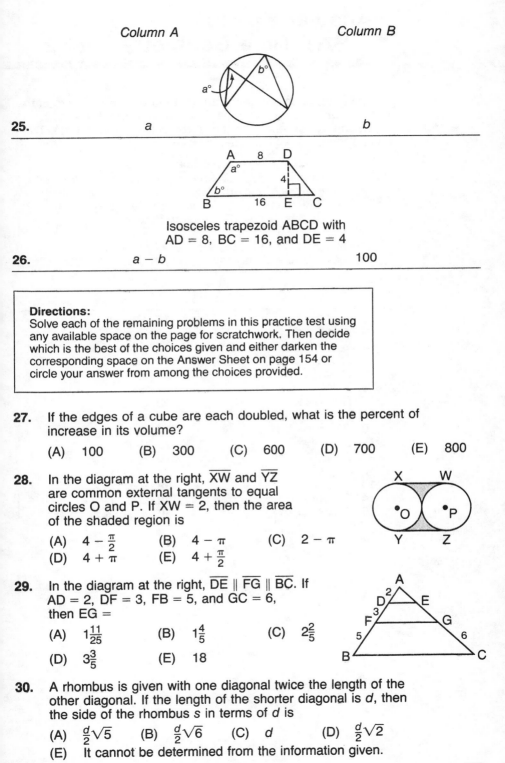

	Column A		Column B

25. a b

Isosceles trapezoid ABCD with
AD = 8, BC = 16, and DE = 4

26. $a - b$ 100

Directions:
Solve each of the remaining problems in this practice test using any available space on the page for scratchwork. Then decide which is the best of the choices given and either darken the corresponding space on the Answer Sheet on page 154 or circle your answer from among the choices provided.

---

27. If the edges of a cube are each doubled, what is the percent of increase in its volume?

(A) 100   (B) 300   (C) 600   (D) 700   (E) 800

28. In the diagram at the right, $\overline{XW}$ and $\overline{YZ}$ are common external tangents to equal circles O and P. If XW = 2, then the area of the shaded region is

(A) $4 - \frac{\pi}{2}$ (B) $4 - \pi$ (C) $2 - \pi$
(D) $4 + \pi$ (E) $4 + \frac{\pi}{2}$

29. In the diagram at the right, $\overline{DE} \parallel \overline{FG} \parallel \overline{BC}$. If AD = 2, DF = 3, FB = 5, and GC = 6, then EG =

(A) $1\frac{11}{25}$ (B) $1\frac{4}{5}$ (C) $2\frac{2}{5}$

(D) $3\frac{3}{5}$ (E) 18

30. A rhombus is given with one diagonal twice the length of the other diagonal. If the length of the shorter diagonal is d, then the side of the rhombus s in terms of d is

(A) $\frac{d}{2}\sqrt{5}$ (B) $\frac{d}{2}\sqrt{6}$ (C) d (D) $\frac{d}{2}\sqrt{2}$
(E) It cannot be determined from the information given.

Answer Key to SAT-Type Geometry Test 2

Following each answer, there is a number or numbers in the form "*a.b*" in parentheses. This number refers to the Geometry Refresher Sections, (beginning on page 23). The first number "*a*" indicates the section.

1. Angles	6. Perimeter
2. Lines	7. Area
3. Polygons	8. Volume
4. Triangles	9. Coordinate Geometry
5. Circles	10. Problem Solving

The number "*b*" indicates the part of the section that explains the rule or method used in solving the problem.

1. C (1.9, 4.3)	**16.** C (3.6)
2. A (1.5, 1.8)	**17.** D (3.6)
3. C (6.1, 3.6)	**18.** C (2.6, 3.6)
4. D (8.1)	**19.** A (7.8)
5. D (4.1, 4.3)	**20.** B (6.3)
6. B (9.5, 4.1)	**21.** B (4.8)
7. C (7.7, 4.8, 6.1)	**22.** C (2.1)
8. D (3.1)	**23.** B (9.5, 7.5)
9. B (4.8, 2.3, 7.1)	**24.** C (4.3)
10. E (4.1, 1.7)	**25.** C (5.7, 5.5)
11. C (4.5, 4.8)	**26.** B (3.6, 4.5, 3.3)
12. D (7.5, 6.2, 7.1)	**27.** D (8.1)
13. A (6.3)	**28.** B (7.1, 7.6)
14. C (5.4)	**29.** D (3.5)
15. E (4.4, 2.4, 2.6)	**30.** A (3.6, 4.8)

Solutions for
SAT-Type Geometry Test 2

1. (C) Since the two angles in a pair of vertical angles are congruent, m $\angle$ ACB = m $\angle$ DCE = 45°. Angles x and y both measure 45° because the sum of the measures of the angles of a triangle is 180°.
Thus, $x + y = 90$.

2. (A) Angles PRS and SRQ are supplementary angles because their exterior sides $\overrightarrow{RP}$ and $\overrightarrow{RQ}$ are opposite rays.
Therefore,
$$z + x - y = 180$$
$$z = 180 - x + y$$

3. (C) If $\frac{3}{8}$ of a side s is 6, then
$$\frac{3}{8}s = 6$$
$$\text{and } \frac{8}{3}\left(\frac{3}{8}s\right) = \frac{8}{3}(6)$$
$$s = 16 \text{ and } P = 4s \text{ or } 64$$

4. (D) The volume V of a rectangular prism is equal to the product of the area of its base B and its height h. The base is a rectangle, so
$$B = \ell w$$
$$B = 3\left(\frac{2}{3}\right) \quad (8 \text{ in.} = \frac{2}{3}\text{ft})$$
$$B = 2 \text{ ft}^2$$
Therefore,
$$V = Bh$$
$$2 = 2(h)$$
$$1 = h$$

5. (D) A right triangle is a triangle with a 90° angle. Since the sum of the measures of the angles of a triangle is 180°, the triangle cannot have an angle which measures 110°.

6. (B) ABC is a right isosceles triangle with CB = AB = 2. The x-coordinate of point A is the same as the x-coordinate of point B.
The y-coordinate must be 2 since the distance AB is 2.
Thus, the coordinates of point A are (2, 2).

7. (C) The area A of a regular polygon is half the product of its apothem a and its perimeter p or $A = \frac{1}{2}ap$. The apothem is the perpendicular bisector of a side and forms a 30-60-90 triangle in a regular hexagon. The length of the apothem is $\frac{1}{2}(2)\sqrt{3} = \sqrt{3}$ and the perimeter of the regular hexagon is 12.

Therefore,
$$A = \tfrac{1}{2}ap$$
$$A = \tfrac{1}{2}(\sqrt{3})(12)$$
$$A = 6\sqrt{3}$$

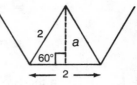

8. (D) If you flip the figure on the left and rotate it so that the marked angles correspond in each figure, it follows that the measure of the marked angle is $g°$.

9. (B) ABC is a 45-45-90 triangle and
$$AC = (BC)\sqrt{2}$$
$$AC = (1)\sqrt{2} = \sqrt{2}$$
Since $AD = DC = \frac{\sqrt{2}}{2}$, then
$$DE = (DC)\sqrt{2}$$
$$DE = \left(\frac{\sqrt{2}}{2}\right)\sqrt{2}$$
$$DE = 1$$
$$\frac{\text{Area of shaded region}}{\text{Area of large square}} = \frac{1^2}{2^2} = \frac{1}{4}$$

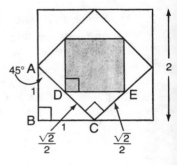

10. (E) Since the acute angles of a right triangle are complementary, it follows that
$$x + a = 90$$
$$b + y = 90$$
From the transitive property of numbers,
$$x + a = b + y$$
Add $-a - y$ to both sides of the equation.
$$x + a - a - y = b + y - a - y$$
$$x - y = b - a$$

11. (C) The altitude in an equilateral triangle is also the bisector of the side to which it is drawn. Therefore, BD = 4. ABD is a 30-60-90 triangle, so $AD = \tfrac{1}{2}(8)\sqrt{3}$ or $AD = 4\sqrt{3}$ and $ED = \tfrac{1}{2}(AD) = \tfrac{1}{2}(4\sqrt{3}) = 2\sqrt{3}$.

Apply the Pythagorean theorem.
$$(BE)^2 = (ED)^2 + (BD)^2$$
$$(BE)^2 = (2\sqrt{3})^2 + 4^2$$
$$(BE)^2 = 12 + 16 = 28$$
$$BE = \sqrt{28}$$

12. (D) Use the formula for the area of an equilateral triangle.
$$A = \frac{s^2}{4}\sqrt{3}$$
$$16\sqrt{3} = \frac{s^2}{4}\sqrt{3}$$
$$64 = s^2$$
$$8 = s$$

The perimeter of the triangle is 3(8) = 24. Since the perimeters of the square and triangle are equal, 24 = 4s, so a side of the square is $\frac{24}{4}$ = 6.

Thus, the area of the square is 6^2 = 36.

13. (A) If w represents the width of the rectangle then $w + x$ represents the length.

Then
$$P = 2(\ell + w)$$
$$P = 2(w + x + w)$$
$$P = 2(2w + x)$$
$$P = 4w + 2x$$
$$P - 4w = 2x$$
$$\frac{P}{2} - 2w = x$$

14. (C) Since the circle is inscribed in the triangle, the sides of the triangle are tangent to the circle. These tangents drawn to the circle from a point outside the circle are congruent. See the diagram.

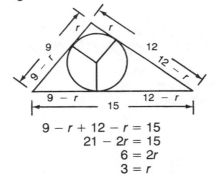

Thus,
$$9 - r + 12 - r = 15$$
$$21 - 2r = 15$$
$$6 = 2r$$
$$3 = r$$

15. (E) △ ABD ≅ △ ACD by SSS, so ∠ BAD ≅ ∠ DAC. Therefore, △ ABE ≅ △ ACE by SAS so m ∠ AEB = m ∠ AEC. If two adjacent angles have their exterior sides lying on a straight line, they are supplementary.
Since m ∠ AEB + m ∠ AEC = 180 and
m ∠ AEB = m ∠ AEC it follows that
m ∠ AEB = m ∠ AEC = 90 and I is true.

△ ABC ≅ △ BCD by SSS, so II must be true.

ACDB is a parellelogram since the four sides are congruent. If $\overline{AC} \parallel \overline{BD}$, then the alternate interior angles of parallel lines are congruent. Thus, ∠ ACB ≅ ∠ CBD, and III is true.

16. (C) Draw line segments AC and BD to form quadrilateral ABCD. If two sides of a quadrilateral are congruent $(\overline{AB} \cong \overline{CD})$ and parallel $(\overline{AB} \parallel \overline{CD})$, the figure is a parallelogram. The opposite sides of a parallelogram are congruent, so $\overline{AC} \cong \overline{BD}$.

17. (D) With the information as given in the problem, either diagram could be drawn. Thus, the relationship cannot be determined.

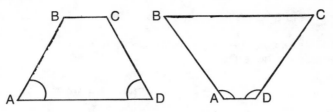

18. (C) If $a = b$, then $\overline{AC} \parallel \overline{BD}$ since a pair of corresponding angles are congruent. Therefore, ABDC is a parallelogram and $\overline{AC} \cong \overline{BD}$ since the opposite sides of a parallelogram are congruent.

19. (A) The side face has an area of $2 \times 3 = 6$, the front face has an area of $5 \times 2 = 10$, and the bottom face has an area of $5 \times 3 = 15$. The sum is $6 + 10 + 15 = 31$. The other three faces form an identical set of faces so the total surface area is $2(31) = 62$.

The area of each face of the cube is $3 \times 3 = 9$.
There are 6 identical faces so the total surface area is $6 \times 9 = 54$.

20. (B) The perimeter of the square is $4(6) = 24$.
The perimeter of the rectangle is
$$P = 2 \,(\ell + w)$$
$$P = 2 \,(9 + 4)$$
$$P = 26$$

21. (B) Apply the Pythagorean theorem with legs of 6 and 7 and hypotenuse of x.
$$x^2 = 6^2 + 7^2$$
$$x^2 = 36 + 49 = 85$$
$$x = \sqrt{85}$$
Thus, $9 < \sqrt{85} < 10$.

22. (C) $BD = CD + 7$ and $BD = BC + CD$, so substitute $BC + CD$ for BD.
$$BC + CD = CD + 7$$
$$BC = 7$$

Substitute 7 for BC.
$$BC = \frac{AC}{2}$$
$$7 = \frac{AC}{2}$$
$$14 = AC$$

Therefore, $AB = AC - BC = 14 - 7 = 7$ and $CD = AD - AC = 21 - 14 = 7$.

23. (B) The base $\overline{AB}$ of the triangle has length $2a$. The height of the triangle has length 4 from the coordinates of point C. Use the formula for the area of a triangle.

$$A = \frac{1}{2} bh$$

$$12 = \frac{1}{\cancel{2}} (\cancel{2}a)\, 4$$

$$12 = 4a$$

$$3 = a$$

24. (C) Let $(x)°$, $(2x)°$, and $(3x)°$ represent the measures of the three angles of the triangle.

$$x + 2x + 3x = 180$$

$$6x = 180$$

$$x = 30$$

$$2x = 60$$

$$3x = 90$$

25. (C) Both angles are inscribed in the same arc and are congruent.

26. (B) Draw altitudes $\overline{AF}$ and $\overline{DE}$. AD = FE = 8. Since the trapezoid is isosceles, BF = EC.

$$BF + FE + EC = 16$$

$$8 + 2(BF) = 16$$

$$2(BF) = 8$$

$$BF = 4$$

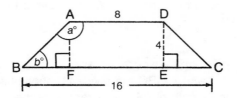

Since AF = BF = 4, $\triangle$ ABF is isosceles. Therefore, $b = 45$ and $a = 180 - 45 = 135$.
Thus, $a - b = 135 - 45 = 90$.

27. (D) If the length of each side of the original cube was e, then the length of each side of the new cube is $2e$. Thus, the original volume was e^3, while the new volume is $(2e)^3$, or $8e^3$. The increase is $7e^3$, or 700% of the original volume.

If your choice was
(A), you found $(2e)^3$ as $2e^3$, which is a 100% increase.
(B), you used $V = e^2$ instead of $V = e^3$.
(C), you used $V = 2e^3$ and $V = 8e^3$ to find the percent of increase.
(E), you found $V = 8e^3$ and did not subtract the original volume.

28. (B) Line segments $\overline{XY}$ and $\overline{WZ}$ will pass through the center of circles O and P forming square XYZW. Since OP = 2, the radius of each circle is 1.

The area of square XYZW = (2)² or 4.

The area of each circle is $\pi r^2 = \pi(1)^2 = \pi$.

The area of the two semicircles enclosed in square XYZW = π.

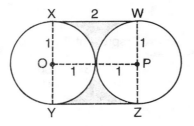

Therefore,
$$\frac{\text{Area of shaded}}{\text{region}} = \text{Area of square} - \frac{\text{Area of two}}{\text{semicircles}}$$
$$= 4 - \pi$$

If your choice was

(A), you found the area of only one semicircle.

(C), you forgot to square the side of length 2.

(D), you added the areas of the semicircles to the area of the square.

(E), you added the area of one semicircle to the area of the square.

29. (D) Since $\overline{DE} \parallel \overline{FG} \parallel \overline{BC}$, $\triangle ADE \sim \triangle AFG \sim \triangle ABC$ and the sides of $\triangle AFG$ and $\triangle ABC$ are divided proportionally. Let y represent the length of $\overline{AE}$ and x represent the length of $\overline{EG}$.

$$\frac{AD}{DF} = \frac{AE}{EG} \qquad \frac{AF}{FB} = \frac{AG}{GC} \qquad (AE + EG = AG)$$
$$\frac{2}{3} = \frac{y}{x} \qquad \frac{5}{5} = \frac{y + x}{6}$$
$$2x = 3y \qquad y + x = 6$$

Solve the equations simultaneously by substitution. Since $y + x = 6$, substitute $6 - x$ for y in $2x = 3y$.

$$2x = 3(6 - x)$$
$$2x = 18 - 3x$$
$$5x = 18$$
$$x = 3\frac{3}{5}$$

If your choice was

(A), you used the proportion $\frac{AD}{FB} = \frac{AG}{GC}$.

(B), you used the proportion $\frac{AF}{AB} = \frac{AG}{GC}$.

166

(C), you used the proportion $\frac{2}{3} = \frac{x}{y}$.

(E), you solved $y + x = 6$ as $y = x - 6$.

30. (A) Let d represent the length of diagonal $\overline{AC}$ and $2d$ represent the length of $\overline{BD}$. Since the diagonals of a rhombus bisect and are perpendicular to each other, $AE = \frac{d}{2}$, $BE = d$, and $m \angle AEB = 90°$.

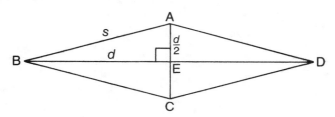

Apply the Pythagorean theorem to $\triangle ABE$.

$$s^2 = d^2 + \left(\frac{d}{2}\right)^2$$
$$s^2 = d^2 + \frac{d^2}{4}$$
$$s^2 = \frac{5d^2}{4}$$
$$s = \frac{d}{2}\sqrt{5}$$

If your choice was

(B), you squared $\left(\frac{d}{2}\right)^2$ as $\frac{d^2}{2}$.

(C), you found the sum of $d^2 + \frac{d^2}{4}$ as d^2.

(D), you found the sum of $d^2 + \frac{d^2}{4}$ as $\frac{d^2}{2}$.

(É), see the solution above.